YOUR STORY IS YOUR POWER

FREE YOUR FEMININE VOICE

ELLE LUNA AND SUSIE HERRICK

WORKMAN PUBLISHING · NEW YORK

Library of Congress Cataloging-in-Publication Data is available.

ISBN 978-1-5235-0269-1

Design by Elle Luna and Lisa Hollander

Workman books are available at special discounts when purchased in bulk for premiums and sales promotions as well as for fund-raising or educational use. Special editions or book excerpts can also be created to specification. For details, contact the Special Sales Director at the address below, or send an email to specialmarkets@ workman.com.

Workman Publishing Co., Inc.
225 Varick Street
New York, NY 10014-4381

workman.com

WORKMAN is a registered trademark of Workman Publishing Co., Inc.

Printed in Hong Kong

First printing January 2018

10 9 8 7 6 5 4 3 2 1

TO THE MEMORY OF ADUPA

and

FOR GERALD O. BARNEY

WHO SHARED HER STORY POWERFULLY BECAUSE
HE ENVISIONED A BETTER FUTURE

"We are volcanoes.
When we women offer our
experience as our truth,
as human truth, all the maps change.
There are new mountains.
That's what I want—
—— to hear you
ERUPTING.
You young Mount St. Helenses who
don't know the power in you—
I want
to hear you."

URSULA K. LE GUIN
AUTHOR

"WE SHALL NOT CEASE FROM EXPLORATION
AND THE END OF ALL OUR EXPLORING
WILL BE TO ARRIVE WHERE WE STARTED
AND KNOW THE PLACE FOR THE FIRST TIME."

T. S. ELIOT
POET

Whether we realize it or not, we define ourselves through stories. Understanding your own story is the key to understanding yourself, your world, and your capacity to act within that world.

In the heart of your story, you will find *you*—your voice, your power, and your truth. And because there is only one you, and you are unique in all of time, your story can be known and expressed only by you. And we need your story—your point of view—and your feminine power now more than ever.

We are at a juncture where we need women's voices, women's intelligence, women's compassion, and women's courage to help us navigate the difficult challenges that our species and our planet face. We use the word "woman" to apply to anyone who identifies with being a woman, regardless of their birth sex. When we say "feminine," we are speaking to the feminine energy that lives in everyone. It is our deepest hope that this book will guide you to the center of your story so that you can share your voice and your true gifts with the world.

The labyrinth is an ancient metaphor for this journey, and it is the organizing principle for this book.

The point of
a maze is to
find its center.
The point of
a labyrinth
is to find
your center.

In a labyrinth, there are no roadblocks or tricky turns. The path flows continuously, like water, spiraling and meandering as it goes. It is not a direct line from one point to another, but an organic, evolving process that takes time and moves to its own rhythm. Similarly, the path through this book is designed to help you spiral to the center of your story and then out again, giving you ways to digest what you discover and to create space for new insights to emerge.

May the meandering, renewing, and turning path of your story continue to guide you—as it has guided us—home.

With love,
Elle and Susie

PART ONE
HOW WE GOT HERE

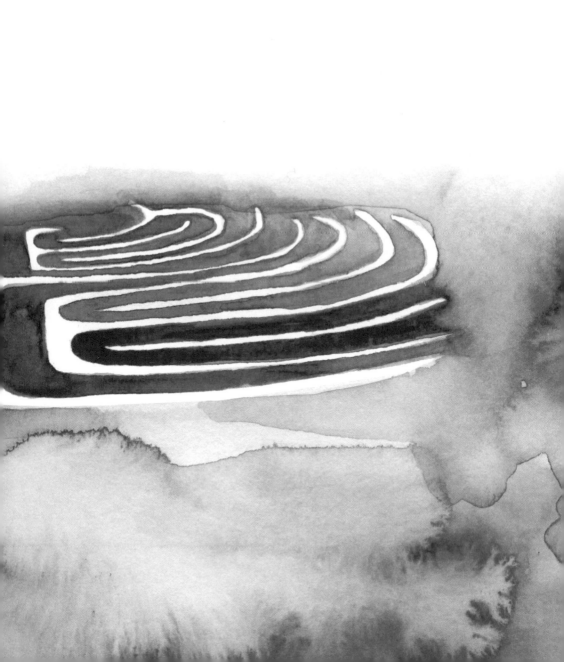

"THE MOST POWERFUL PERSON IN THE WORLD IS THE STORYTELLER.... THE STORYTELLER SETS THE VISION, VALUES & AGENDA OF AN ENTIRE GENERATION THAT IS TO COME."

STEVE JOBS

AS RECOUNTED BY TOMAS HIGBEY, JOURNALIST

STORIES LIVE INSIDE YOU AND SHAPE YOUR LIFE. BUT WHY?

What were the earliest stories you heard that hooked you? What compelled you to want to hear them again and again? What inspired you to share them with others—perhaps even your own children—passing those stories on throughout time, giving the stories life?

The most enduring tales tap into something larger than mere entertainment: They literally help us *evolve*.

We warm our hands on stories—both historical and imagined—all the while taking in essential information:

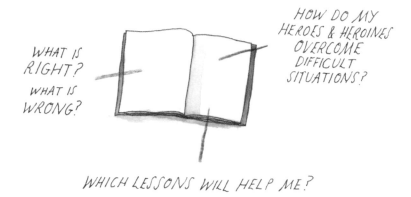

WHAT IS RIGHT?
WHAT IS WRONG?

HOW DO MY HEROES & HEROINES OVERCOME DIFFICULT SITUATIONS?

WHICH LESSONS WILL HELP ME?

The sharing of fairy tales from generation to generation is among the most enduring methods for creating and sustaining culture. What does that mean for us?

For women, much of our early collective education resides in these tales. It is as though each of us is given a recipe that shows us what to do to create a successful life, as well as how to behave to get that life. The characters, attributes, and themes of these well-known tales socialize us from a very young age, shaping our earliest ideas of who we are, what our culture values in us, and who we feel we ought to become if we want to find our own *happily ever after*. As women throughout time grapple with the directives for *happily ever after*, we watch the story, we learn from the story, and, unless challenged, we will, in time, live the story. So what's the story?

For girls, the earliest and oldest story is often a fairy tale. What young girl or woman today isn't intimately familiar with "Cinderella"? "Beauty and the Beast"? "Snow White"?

In the classic fairy tale "Cinderella," a beloved daughter is orphaned, adopted, and turned into an indentured servant while everyone else gets to go to the ball. With the help of a fairy godmother, a dress, and a famous pair of shoes, Cinderella goes to the ball and is so beautiful that the handsome young prince falls in love with her. Despite the jealousy of her stepmother and stepsisters, Cinderella gets the prince, becomes a princess, and is lifted out of her painful life of manual labor.

Recipe for Belle, in *Beauty and the Beast*

☐ SACRIFICE YOURSELF
☐ BE BEAUTIFUL
☐ USE SEXUALITY
☐ BE DEMURE
☐ GET PRINCE

Another classic tale is "Beauty and the Beast." The main character, Belle ("beautiful" in French), is also a beauty. She finds herself in a horrible situation—her beloved father is imprisoned by the cruel, arrogant Beast, so she sacrifices herself and becomes the Beast's prisoner in exchange for her father's release. Beast frightens Belle and is cruel to her, but he develops feelings for her. Trapped in an abusive relationship, Belle uses her beauty, sexuality, and submissive spirit to turn Beast into a kinder man, with whom she eventually falls in love.

Finally, "Snow White." Like the other women, Snow White is slim, demure, and physically attractive, but her beauty makes her stepmother jealous. This conflict creates the central plot of the story: Multiple attempts are made to murder the girl—asphyxiating her with a corset, putting out a bounty on her head, and, finally, poisoning an apple, of which Snow White takes a bite. Ultimately, a handsome young man (who also happens to be a prince) falls in love with the girl because, once again, she is beautiful. He kisses her while she is unconscious— obviously without her consent—and brings her back to life.

WHEN A
POPULAR
DEMOTE
BEAUTIFUL
WHAT DOES A
BEGIN TO FEEL
VALUES

CULTURE'S MOST STORIES WOMEN TO HOUSEKEEPERS, YOUNG GIRL SOCIETY IN HER?

With the main plot points laid out plainly, we can't help but wonder why these foundational stories are centered on a woman who has no capacity to take care of herself and needs a prince to come take care of her.

As women, do we see that these fairy tales are a part of the brainwashing of women? Do we call the bluff? Do we write our own children's books or craft our own nursery rhymes? As girls, are we simply too young to know any better? Do we begin to believe that we need to strive to be like Cinderella? Do we get carried along in the fun songs and the parts that we do like, all the while sweeping the stories that don't seem quite right under the rug?

We might not like to think we're susceptible to conditioning from something as innocent as a fairy tale, but children learn from everything—especially stories that are intriguing or entertaining.

In the early 1900s, Edward Bernays, a nephew of Sigmund Freud, used some of his uncle's ideas to subconsciously manipulate the people who viewed advertisements. It involved crowd psychology. Upon studying motivations that led people to do what "the crowd" was doing, he discovered that if the most beautiful and powerful people were doing something, others would subconsciously want to do it, too.

This breakthrough was then applied to the cigarette industry and to women, specifically, because they smoked far less than men. His first strategy was to encourage women to smoke instead of eat, celebrating images of thin women and gaining doctors' endorsements that said smoking was better for you than eating sweets.

"To stay slender - reach for a cigarette."

The next step was to suggest, through imagery, that men oppressed women and that smoking cigarettes publicly would signify freedom. The cigarettes were branded as "Torches of Freedom," which they hoped women would proudly display and consume in public. They did—in mass numbers.

Years later, the author and activist Naomi Wolf examined the effects of these messages on women. In a research study, women were shown advertisements that featured women of various appearances, sizes, and ages and were asked, "Who is the most attractive?" The overwhelming majority of participants pointed to the women who adhered to unrealistic, unhealthy, and compulsory ideas of beauty.

"OUR SOCIETY DOES REWARD BEAUTY ON THE OUTSIDE OVER HEALTH ON THE INSIDE... A THIN YOUNG WOMAN WITH PRECANCEROUS LUNGS [WHO SMOKES TO STAY THIN] IS MORE HIGHLY REWARDED SOCIALLY THAN A HEARTY OLD CRONE."

NAOMI WOLF
AUTHOR

These stories aren't new, and they aren't limited to Disney or even to the last one hundred years. But if it's so obvious to see how we have been conditioned, then why don't we simply choose to do something different?

When so many messages are imprinted from an early, impressionable age—from how we should behave to achieve a fairy-tale ending to how we are supposed to look to be considered beautiful—it seems that no matter how conscious an adult each of us grows up to be, we find ourselves tied to the fairy tale.

But like any good science-fiction story where the heroine or the hero starts to figure out what's going on just in time to correct course, many women, and some men, are beginning to realize that roughly half of the human race is being manipulated.

WOMEN ARE BEGINNING TO SEE THE DIRE NEED TO TAKE THE STORY AWAY FROM THE STORYTELLERS AND BRING IT BACK TO US.

PART TWO

HOW YOU GOT HERE

"I NEED TO LISTEN WELL SO THAT I HEAR WHAT IS NOT SAID."

THULI MADONSELA
SOUTH AFRICAN ADVOCATE

IN ORDER TO TAKE BACK YOUR STORY
YOU FIRST MUST KNOW YOURSELF.

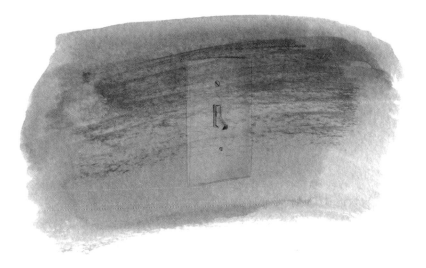

Becoming more aware is a process akin to looking for a light switch
in a dark room. You might pass your hands over the dark walls for
a long time, or you might find the switch rather quickly. But either
way, once you find the switch, the lights go on in a way that shifts your
perception of everything. You can never *unsee* once you see. And with
this newfound understanding, you receive the greatest gift of all—*choice*
about how you want your life to unfold.

The path to seeing the fullness of your story starts with recalling memories, experiences, and the important twists and turns you made along the way, even as your story continues to unfold. While writing down your story might seem like a large task, think of it as a discerning road map that will keep you from going down rabbit holes and getting lost in random minutiae. The benefits:

YOU WILL BECOME MORE AWARE OF WHAT HAS AFFECTED YOUR EMOTIONAL LIFE.

GET TO KNOW YOUR

YOU WILL GAIN AWARENESS ABOUT HOW YOU FELT YOU OUGHT TO BEHAVE, AND YOU'LL GET TO OBSERVE AND EVALUATE WHETHER OR NOT THOSE BEHAVIORS ARE IN YOUR BEST INTEREST NOW.

YOU WILL IDENTIFY YOUR BLOCKS, AND YOU WILL GET TO DECIDE IF THEY ARE HELPING OR HINDERING YOU FROM MOVING TOWARD THE LIFE THAT YOU CRAVE.

STORY

YOU WILL DEVELOP A FRIENDLY AWARENESS OF YOURSELF, ALSO CALLED A THIRD-PARTY OBSERVER, AND THIS OBSERVER WILL BE A COMPASSIONATE HELPMATE AS YOU NAVIGATE YOUR JOURNEY.

Your story is composed of three intersecting narratives: your cultural story, your family's story, and your personal story. Let's start with the largest of the three contexts—the cultural story.

"THE TRUTH WILL SET YOU FREE, BUT FIRST IT WILL PISS YOU OFF."

AS QUOTED BY
GLORIA STEINEM
ACTIVIST

YOUR CULTURAL STORY

We all get our opinions from somewhere, but we might not know exactly where or how. In order to understand the impact of your culture on your story, start by answering some questions:

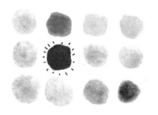

HOW DO YOU FEEL YOU ARE TREATED IN LIGHT OF YOUR CULTURE, COUNTRY OF BIRTH, GENDER, RELIGION, OR OTHER DISTINCTIVE FACTORS?

HOW ARE OTHERS, WHO ARE LIKE YOU, TREATED?

As you start to identify and understand the patterns that show up around you, you will begin to see the cultural impact on your own story. It is usually the *unsaid* or *unseen* that impacts our psyche the most because we blindly adhere to memes that we are not conscious of.

WHAT BELIEFS DO YOU HAVE ABOUT POLITICS, MARRIAGE, CHILD REARING, AND EDUCATION, OR ANY OTHER CULTURAL INFLUENCERS THAT LEAP TO MIND?

Some of the cultural categories that can impact you are race, religion, country of origin, age, economic status, and sex. The most pervasive and unseen cultural impact on women's lives is how they have been treated by society because they are female.

Patriarchy is the dominant world paradigm, and it affects every woman.

a society or system of government in which men hold the power, and women are largely excluded from it.

By definition, patriarchy is a hierarchy. There are many types of hierarchies, and some of them are necessary and helpful. For example, you wouldn't want a summer intern in charge of building a spaceship engine that will send astronauts into outer space. You also wouldn't want to lose the classifications and hierarchies within the animal kingdom because it's a helpful way for us to understand the food chain. But hierarchies stop being helpful the instant one group subordinates another group in the name of authority, domination, or power. These types of hierarchies are sustained, as Gandhi observed, through humiliation of the dominated group. When this happens, these systems become hierarchies rooted in oppression, and patriarchy is one of these hierarchies because it is built on the oppression of women.

From a very young age, girls are exposed to countless messages that reinforce this notion that men are the "head of the house" and women must obey. As a result, men are given more resources, have more cultural authority, and are not held to the same cultural expectations as women.

PATRIARCHY

MEN
HOLD PRIMARY
POWER IN FAMILY,
GOVERNMENT,
RELIGION, AND SOCIETY

WOMEN
DO NOT

IT'S JUST LOCKER ROOM TALK.

ALL MEN DO THIS.

NOT UNDER YOUR FATHER'S ROOF.

BOYS WILL
BE BOYS.

DON'T DO
ANYTHING TO
MAKE YOUR
FATHER ANGRY.

The most insidious side effect of patriarchy is misogyny. While sexism is a prejudice or stereotype on the basis of sex, misogyny is defined as the *hatred* of women. More specifically, misogyny can manifest as:

INDIFFERENCE TO WOMEN'S NEEDS

AGGRESSIVE ATTEMPTS TO COERCE OR KEEP WOMEN CONTROLLED

ENJOYMENT OF WOMEN'S MISFORTUNE OR OPPRESSION

The psychological effects of cultural misogyny on girls are astounding. By the time a young girl is six or seven years old, she has already begun to formulate an internal template based on the countless impressions that have told her men are superior to women. If these impressions are left in the unconscious, these girls could grow up to be women who suffer from a range of psychological disorders.

If the psychological impact of patriarchy on women is so well documented, and if almost every woman currently alive is born into patriarchy, why haven't things shifted already? Why is this trio of patriarchy, sexism, and misogyny still here?

LEARNED HELPLESSNESS, INTERGENERATIONAL POST-TRAUMATIC STRESS DISORDER, AN OVERWHELMING FEAR OF HOMICIDE & ABUSE, ACUTE STRESS & ANXIETY, LOW SELF-ESTEEM, DEPRESSION, MIGRAINES (OR OTHER EXTERNAL REFLECTIONS OF AN INTERNAL DISCORDANT TEMPLATE), WOUNDED RELATIONSHIP BETWEEN INTERNAL MASCULINE & FEMININE, SPLITTING (WHERE SOMEONE IS ALL GOOD OR ALL BAD AND THERE IS NO MIDDLE GROUND), CONTINUED EMBODIMENT AND REINFORCEMENT OF THE PATRIARCHY & INTERNALIZED MISOGYNY (MEANING THAT THE MISOGYNY IS DIRECTED INWARD AT THE SELF)

"WE ARE LIKE CHALLENGED TO SINCE THE FISH HAS ANYTHING ELSE, FOR IT TO SEE OR CONCEIVE BUT A

FISH UNDERSTAND WATER: NEVER EXPERIENCED

IT IS ALMOST IMPOSSIBLE OF THE WATER. BUBBLE RISING PAST THE INQUISITIVE FISH CAN OFFER A CRITICAL CLUE. »

DAVID EAGLEMAN
NEUROSCIENTIST

WHERE DID MISOGYNY BEGIN?

The origins of misogyny are debatable. While some say it is five thousand years old, starting as early as the origin of writing and commerce, others believe that it is as old as human culture, and stems from the belief that since women can create human life, they must be oppressed to keep them from dominating men. What we do know is that it is a worldwide phenomenon that has been expressed consistently and horribly throughout history.

Was there ever a time in history where women held equal positions with men? Or have we ever had a society where women were in charge? Historians don't know, but what is evident is that there have been periods in history where women have had wildly different statuses, ranging from being considered nonhuman (meaning they held the same status as animals) to being the leaders of empires.

Here are a few things that have been said about women throughout history by individuals you might recognize:

"THE FEMINIST AGENDA IS NOT ABOUT EQUAL RIGHTS FOR WOMEN. IT IS ABOUT A SOCIALIST, ANTI-FAMILY POLITICAL MOVEMENT THAT ENCOURAGES WOMEN TO LEAVE THEIR HUSBANDS, KILL THEIR CHILDREN, PRACTICE WITCHCRAFT, DESTROY CAPITALISM, AND BECOME LESBIANS."
— PAT ROBERTSON, SOUTHERN BAPTIST MINISTER & BROADCASTER

"WHEN A WOMAN HAS SCHOLARLY INCLINATIONS THERE IS USUALLY SOMETHING WRONG WITH HER SEXUAL ORGANS."
— FRIEDRICH NIETZSCHE

"NATURE INTENDED WOMEN TO BE OUR SLAVES. THEY ARE OUR PROPERTY."
— NAPOLEON BONAPARTE

"WOMAN IS A TEMPLE BUILT OVER A SEWER." TERTULLIAN

"GO TO HELL, I'LL NEVER HAVE MY FILL OF HATING WOMEN, NOT IF I'M SAID TO TALK WITHOUT CEASING. FOR WOMEN ARE ALSO UNCEASINGLY WICKED. EITHER SOMEONE SHOULD TEACH THEM TO BE SENSIBLE, OR LET ME TRAMPLE THEM UNDERFOOT FOREVER."
— EURIPIDES, FROM THE PLAY HIPPOLYTA

33

"THE RELATION OF MALE TO FEMALE IS BY NATURE A RELATION OF SUPERIOR TO INFERIOR AND RULER TO RULED."

PLATO

"IT IS BETTER FOR YOU TO HAVE PUT YOUR MANHOOD IN THE MOUTH OF A VENOMOUS SNAKE OR A PIT OF BURNING CHARCOAL THAN A WOMAN."

—BUDDHA GOTAMA

"GRAB THEM BY THE PUSSY.

"THE FEMALE ALSO IS MORE SUBJECT TO DEPRESSION...AND DESPAIR THAN THE MALE. SHE IS ALSO MORE SHAMELESS AND FALSE, MORE READILY DECEIVED."

—ARISTOTLE

"I DON'T THINK THERE IS ANYTHING PARTICULARLY WRONG ABOUT HITTING A WOMAN—ALTHOUGH I DON'T RECOMMEND DOING IT IN THE SAME WAY YOU'D HIT A MAN. AN OPENHANDED SLAP IS JUSTIFIED—IF ALL OTHER ALTERNATIVES FAIL AND THERE HAS BEEN PLENTY OF WARNING. IF A WOMAN IS A BITCH, OR HYSTERICAL, OR BLOODY-MINDED CONTINUALLY, THEN I'D DO IT. I THINK A MAN HAS TO BE SLIGHTLY ADVANCED, AHEAD OF THE WOMAN."

—SIR SEAN CONNERY

"THE WORD AND WORKS OF GOD IS QUITE CLEAR, THAT WOMEN WERE MADE EITHER TO BE WIVES OR PROSTITUTES."
— MARTIN LUTHER

"FEMINISM WAS ESTABLISHED SO AS TO ALLOW UNATTRACTIVE WOMEN ACCESS TO THE MAINSTREAM OF SOCIETY."
— RUSH LIMBAUGH

"WIVES, SUBMIT YOURSELVES TO YOUR OWN HUSBANDS."
— THE BIBLE

"YOU CAN DO ANYTHING."
— DONALD TRUMP

"TO THE WOMAN HE SAID, 'I WILL MAKE YOUR PAINS IN CHILDBEARING VERY SEVERE; WITH PAINFUL LABOR YOU WILL GIVE BIRTH TO CHILDREN; YET YOUR DESIRE WILL BE FOR YOUR HUSBAND, AND HE WILL RULE OVER YOU."

THE BIBLE

Misogyny is embedded in the culture and can be hard to see.

"WHEN [SUPREME COURT JUSTICE RUTH BADER GINSBURG] WENT TO LAW SCHOOL AT COLUMBIA IN THE 1950s, THERE WERE NO WOMEN'S BATHROOMS IN THE BUILDING. 'IF NATURE CALLED, YOU HAD TO MAKE A MAD DASH TO ANOTHER BUILDING THAT HAD A WOMEN'S BATHROOM,' SHE RECALLED...

IT WAS 'EVEN WORSE IF YOU WERE IN THE MIDDLE OF AN EXAM. WE NEVER COMPLAINED; IT NEVER OCCURRED TO US TO COMPLAIN.'"

JUSTICE RUTH BADER GINSBURG

AS RECOUNTED BY SHANKAR VEDANTAM

IN THE HIDDEN BRAIN

37

Oftentimes, when men display solidarity or identification with something seen as overly feminine, they receive social backlash. For example, one of the biggest insults a man can say to another man is to refer to him as "a girl." Or, if they agree with their wives or are doing something to be of service to them, they might be called "pussy-whipped." This keeps men separated from women, making intimacy almost impossible. The more aware men become, the more they realize the effect it has on them. Men are starting to realize that women deal with misogyny all the time:

"WOMEN ARE RESPONSIBLE FOR TWO-THIRDS OF THE WORK DONE WORLDWIDE, YET EARN ONLY TEN PERCENT OF THE TOTAL INCOME AND OWN ONE PERCENT OF THE TOTAL PROPERTY... SO, ARE WE EQUALS? UNTIL THE ANSWER IS YES, WE MUST NEVER STOP ASKING."

— DANIEL CRAIG
ACTOR

WORK   EARNINGS   PROPERTY

As a woman born (most likely) into patriarchal culture, the most important questions to ask yourself as you consider your own cultural story are:

HOW HAVE YOU BEEN IMPACTED BY A GLOBAL CULTURE THAT VALUES AND EMPOWERS MEN ABOVE WOMEN?

How have you been impacted by your national culture? Your race? Your socioeconomic status? The spiritual culture that you were born into?

We—Susie and Elle—each discovered that we had internalized cultural misogyny.

SUSIE

After a big breakup, I had a life-changing epiphany. I noticed that whenever I had a boyfriend, I felt great and had life by the tail. But whenever I was single, I felt inferior to others and ashamed. This inspired me to sit down with a friend at a restaurant and quickly jot down what came to mind when I thought about women. As I wrote on my placemat, I realized that deep down, I didn't really feel that I was a person at all because I was a woman. Rather, I felt like my existence was conditional. I was alive only to be beautiful and/or to procreate. And if I didn't do that? I needed to be rich. Other than that, I was useless. I continued writing these things down, and once they were collected on the placemat, I studied them through my lens as a trained psychotherapist. This groundbreaking moment was my first real, conscious experience of uncovering my own internal misogyny. After that day, I intervened on my own behalf and began to transform my internal misogynist from a dominant oppressor into an inner masculine partner that would stand up for me and believe in my innate gifts as a woman.

ELLE

My journey with misogyny began when I started listening to the little
voice in my mind that I called my "inner critic." This voice would
pop up while I was painting, or getting dressed, or driving . . . or
doing anything, really. But as I began to listen to this "inner critic,"
I realized that *critic* was an understatement. The voice was much worse
than critical—it was downright hateful to me simply because I had been
born a woman. It told me that I should never age, I should never rock
the boat, and I should never speak out on my own behalf because it
might make others upset. To listen to this internal voice playing on
repeat in my mind was painful, but by bringing it into consciousness,
I could begin to talk to it and, with time, transform it. As the
psychologist Carl Rogers once said, "The curious paradox is
that when I accept myself just as I am, then I can change."

For both of us, bringing misogyny and its effects on our own minds
into consciousness changed the course of our lives in unimaginably
positive ways.

YOUR CULTURAL STORY

CULTURAL MESSAGES

↓

AS A WOMAN

How do messages you have received from others about being a woman impact your life? For example:

DO YOU FEEL EMPOWERED TO CONFRONT A BOSS IF YOU ARE BEING PAID UNEQUALLY?

WERE YOU TREATED DIFFERENTLY IN YOUR FAMILY BECAUSE YOU WERE FEMALE?

HAS ANYONE EVER TAKEN CREDIT FOR YOUR IDEAS?

HAVE YOU EVER BACKED OFF FROM A COMPETITION BECAUSE MEN WERE IN THE RUNNING?

DO YOU THINK YOU'RE PRETTY? HOW DOES THAT AFFECT YOUR INTERACTIONS?

HAVE YOU EVER FELT SO EMBARRASSED THAT IT CHANGED YOU AND/ OR YOUR COURSE OF ACTION IN A SIGNIFICANT WAY?

Consider doing some research on how additional aspects of your culture have affected you. For example, you can investigate the history of your country or religion, or look at current culturally biased messages that you see modeled in your own behavior and the behavior of the people around you.

→ SPIRITUAL, RACIAL, & SOCIOECONOMIC

Ask yourself the following questions:

- *Where did my parents come from?*
- *What religion was I raised in?*
- *What religion am I now?*
- *Does religion matter to me?*
- *What race am I?*
- *What impact does the fact that I am a particular race have on my interactions with my classmates, workmates, and neighbors?*
- *How are my relatives' lives affected by their socioeconomic status, race, or religion? For example, are they privileged and do they have doors opened for them, or have they struggled? Has my family been shown disrespect?*
- *Are my parents' social lives affected by what they do for a living?*
- *Have I had positive or negative experiences when approaching a club or social group of interest to me?*

YOUR CULTURAL STORY

QUICK ASSOCIATION

This diversity training activity was used by Delorme McKee-Stovall, an advocate for human and civil rights. Speed is key when answering these prompts, so just write down the first thing that comes to mind, without judgment. No one else has to see the answers.

POLITICIANS ARE

_____.

JEWISH PEOPLE ARE

_____.

CONSTRUCTION WORKERS ARE

_____.

STRAIGHT PEOPLE ARE

_____.

CORPORATE PEOPLE ARE

_____.

GAY PEOPLE ARE

_____.

ELDERLY PEOPLE ARE

_____.

TRANS-GENDER PEOPLE ARE

_____.

POLICE OFFICERS ARE

_____.

HISPANIC PEOPLE ARE

_____.

HAIRDRESSERS ARE

_____.

SINGLE MOTHERS ARE

_____.

LEFT-HANDED PEOPLE ARE

_____.

WHITE PEOPLE ARE

_____.

MUSLIM PEOPLE ARE

_____.

PROFESSIONAL BASKETBALL PLAYERS ARE

_____.

YOUR CULTURAL STORY

FOCUS YOUR STORY

Get blank note cards to write down highlights of Your Cultural Story.

Name eight to ten ways that you have been impacted by a global culture that values and empowers men above women. Can you recall memories or experiences where the cultural story directly impacted your life? Write them down, one per card. If you get stuck, go back to the previous exercises and write some of your earlier responses down.

SUSIE:

I REMEMBER WATCHING AN EPISODE OF THE 1960s TV SERIES BATMAN WHERE A "DISASTER" HAPPENED. WOMEN TOOK OVER GOTHAM CITY AND NOTHING COULD GET DONE BECAUSE THEY SAT AROUND LOOKING IN THE MIRROR ALL DAY PUTTING ON LIPSTICK.

What stories, beliefs, images, or memories do you carry with you pertaining to your culture? If they irritated or frustrated you, it's a good sign that you're on the right track.

"IF YOU WANT TO UNDERSTAND ANY WOMAN YOU MUST FIRST ASK HER ABOUT HER MOTHER AND THEN LISTEN CAREFULLY.... THE MORE A DAUGHTER KNOWS ABOUT THE DETAILS OF HER MOTHER'S LIFE... THE STRONGER THE DAUGHTER."

—ANITA DIAMANT
AUTHOR
THE RED TENT

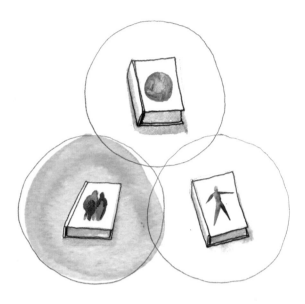

YOUR FAMILY STORY

Have you ever seen a dog circle the ground before lying down to sleep? The dog is exhibiting a behavior based on information inherited from its wolf ancestors that tells the dog if it is going to lie down in tall grass, it must first mat the grass down. A shih tzu in Manhattan who has never seen grass taller than a few inches will still perform this age-old ritual.

Just as you are born into a broad cultural story, you are also a part of your family's ongoing narrative. Psychiatrist and professor Murray Bowen learned that, like the dog, we transmit some behaviors from one generation to the next. If you want to understand your own story, it's helpful to look at it within the context of your family.

Some questions that a family therapist might ask to understand your family structure are:

WHO WAS IN CHARGE IN YOUR FAMILY? WHY?

DID YOU EXPERIENCE CLOSE FAMILY RELATIONSHIPS WHERE YOU FELT LIKE YOU WERE SMOTHERED?

OR DID YOU FEEL LIKE YOU WEREN'T PARTICULARLY CLOSE TO YOUR FAMILY MEMBERS?

WERE PEOPLE WILLING TO TALK ABOUT THINGS?

DID YOU HAVE PRIVACY?

WHAT WERE THE FAMILY RULES, BOTH EXPLICIT AND IMPLICIT?

DID YOU HAVE ANY FAMILY MYTHS AND/OR BELIEFS?

DID YOUR FAMILY HAVE ANY PARTICULAR TALENTS?

FOR EXAMPLE, ARE PEOPLE IN YOUR FAMILY STORYTELLERS? ATHLETIC? MUSICALLY TALENTED?

49

YOUR FAMILY STORY

LEARN YOUR FAMILY STORY

Interview someone influential in your family and ask them questions— even if you think you already know the answers. This person could be from your family in which you grew up, from the generation before you, or perhaps even one of your own children.

You could ask:

- *What are the family rules around marriage, divorce, or sex?*
- *What were the expectations about becoming pregnant or getting someone else pregnant?*
- *Where do you think those rules came from?*
- *What are some of your early memories about your parents and grandparents?*
- *What traits did they pass down to you?*
- *Where do you think some of these traits came from?*
- *What do you know about your family history? Do you remember interesting stories about your oldest relatives or ancestors?*

As you collect answers, you will start to become more aware of the impact of the process on you:

WITH WHOM DID YOU FEEL MOST COMFORTABLE ASKING THESE QUESTIONS?

WHAT THOUGHTS OR FEELINGS AROSE FOR YOU AS YOU ASKED THESE QUESTIONS?

DID YOU RECORD THEM? WHY OR WHY NOT?

We, Susie and Elle, came from families whose rules about pregnancy were strong and specific.

SUSIE:

I remembered that when I was about five, I used to hit my stomach; I was using my fist to try to loosen up what was inside so a baby couldn't stay in there. I felt sick inside and afraid when I looked in the mirror. It was shocking to realize how, as a child, I had internalized the family/cultural fear that I shouldn't get pregnant before wedlock and how deep the terror went into my psyche way before puberty.

ELLE:

When Susie told me this, I recalled when, as a child, I saw that my stomach stuck out very far, and I assumed that I was pregnant. I wasn't, of course, but looking back all these years later, I recall a poignant sense of dread and shame that I was pregnant. I felt terrified and said nothing about it for years.

YOUR FAMILY STORY

YOU'RE IN THE CAR

You're in the car with your family, and a driver cuts you off. What would each member of your family say when they see that the offending driver is . . .

- *a man wearing a business suit and texting on his phone?*

- *a fashion model wearing a tank top?*

- *an African American teenage boy wearing a do-rag?*

- *an elderly woman clutching the wheel and leaning forward?*

- *an Asian man driving a luxury sedan with tinted windows?*

- *a taxi driver wearing a turban?*

The responses to these exercises might show that certain prejudices have been passed down through generations. By identifying them and bringing them into your consciousness, you are better able to choose whether or not they're working for you in a positive way.

It might be helpful to look at some of the characteristics and beliefs of your family. To help identify them, try answering these questions:

- *What are some of the distinctive characteristics of your family (e.g., are they boisterous, controlled, intellectual, loving)?*

- *Did your family have explicit expectations of you or other family members?*

- *Were there family myths that you discovered or busted later in life?*

- *How would you describe your family to other people?*

- *What are you most proud of about your family?*

- *What are you most ashamed of?*

- *What makes you angry about your family?*

We each looked at our own family history.

ELLE :

I come from a long line of attorneys. As I grew up, I figured
I should be a lawyer, just like them. I applied to nine law
schools, and I was rejected from every single one—even the
safety school. I felt like a total failure. Without any other
option, I paused to really look at my life. Although I had
applied to so many law schools, I was painting around the
clock, practically sleeping at the art studio, and skipping
meals just so I could make art. For some reason, I never
accepted that I could actually pursue my creativity as a way
of life. I had unconsciously assumed that I needed to go to
law school so that I could make money and be secure, even
though I wasn't passionate about law. I kept telling myself
that I could be an intellectual property attorney so that at
least I would get to *work with* artists. Thanks in part to those
rejections, I came to see that my desire to go to law school
stemmed from family messages about what was safe and
valuable. And then I realized that I had the freedom to make
choices that suited me better.

SUSIE:

For reasons I didn't understand for a long time, I've always had an irrational fear of becoming a victim of physical abuse and homicide. It is strange because there is no history of violent abuse in my family, but I could feel it, and I could see a similar terror in the eyes of my female relatives. We all shared a belief that if we made a mistake, or stood out too much, something really bad would happen to us. I decided to go back into my family history to see if there was anything that might explain this fear. Nothing seemed to correlate with the fears until I discovered that there were several relatives in the 1600s who were closely connected to the Salem witch trials. One relative was the constable responsible for arresting the suspects, and another was the marshal who carried out the verdicts. The marshal also served as a witness for the prosecution. Other relatives were on juries or served as witnesses. Most disturbing of all—one of my female ancestors was a suspect. After I uncovered this information, I realized that I had absorbed a hidden message from my family through spoken and unspoken stories, actions, and responses: If you stand out in any way that seems unusual, you will be a suspect, and you may be killed.

YOUR FAMILY STORY

FOCUS YOUR STORY

Get a dozen note cards on which to write down highlights of Your Family Story.

Name eight to ten beliefs and traits that you inherited from your family. They may have been passed down for many generations. Write each of them on its own card.

For example, Susie's family story included these notes: "We are musically talented," "Family sticks together," and "Question authority." What beliefs and traits do you feel you hold as a part of your family history?

AS YOU CONTINUE
TO FIND CLUES ABOUT
WHAT YOU HAVE INHERITED
FROM OTHER GENERATIONS,
YOU WILL BEGIN TO
GET A **SENSE OF HOW**
AND WHY YOU ARE
THE WAY YOU ARE.
IT'S AS THOUGH

YOUR LIFE WILL
START TO OPEN LIKE
A BOOK.

"IF SHE GOT REALLY
QUIET AND LISTENED,
NEW PARTS OF HER
WANTED TO SPEAK."

SARK

AUTHOR AND ARTIST

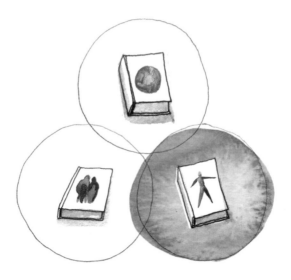

JOUR PERSONAL STORY

To know the story of your life, once you've looked at the cultural influences and after you've identified what your family might have passed on to you, you will want look at your own personality structure so you can evaluate the way it is supporting—or not supporting—you. You may notice that you have a way of maneuvering in the world that is different from that of your siblings or other family members, even though you have the same cultural and family background.

You may think of your personality as just a naturally occurring part of you. But scientists have not yet fully determined how much of personality is intrinsic—just "you"—and how much is learned behavior and responses. What we do know is that both genetics and early experiences affect how we maneuver in the world, and despite how indelible our personalities can feel, the brain remains *neuroplastic*, or "malleable," throughout our lives. The purpose of understanding your personality is to find those aspects that are keeping you from the life that you want.

Looking at how you went about getting your needs met as a baby and a child provides a window into your personality structure.

MAYBE YOU LEARNED VERY EARLY ON THAT IF YOU CRIED, SOMEONE WOULD QUICKLY COME TO YOUR SIDE.

OR PERHAPS THE OPPOSITE WAS TRUE AND YOU LEARNED THAT MAKING YOUR NEEDS KNOWN WAS NOT A WELCOME BEHAVIOR.

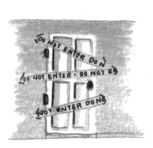

MAYBE YOU LEARNED TO BE DEFENSIVE OR TERRITORIAL TO PROTECT YOUR BELONGINGS FROM YOUR SIBLINGS.

OR PERHAPS YOU BECAME AWARE THAT BY GIVING AWAY YOUR BELONGINGS, OTHERS WOULD LIKE YOU AND EVENTUALLY WOULD BECOME DEPENDENT ON YOU, SECURING YOUR POSITION IN THE FAMILY.

Psychologists study different personality structures and categorize them according to systems called personality typologies. These will help you find your personality type and begin to understand the motivation behind your behavior. As you gradually gain self-awareness, you can begin to observe and evaluate how your personality is functioning. You can start this process with questions like:

WHAT ARE YOUR EARLIEST MEMORIES ABOUT HOW YOU INTERACTED WITH OTHERS?

IN YOUR CHILDHOOD, WHEN DID YOUR INTERNAL CONFLICTS BEGIN?

DID YOU OR ANYONE ELSE SQUELCH YOUR DREAMS? WHEN AND WHY?

There are many ways to learn more about your personality: The
Myers-Briggs Type Indicator is a system you may have heard of. The
system that we use is the Enneagram because of its unique ability
to uncover motivation and help predict behavior. The Enneagram
itself is a geometric figure used to represent the human mind. It is
organized into a system of nine interrelated personality types. While
the whole system is quite intricate and it can take many years of study
to grasp its full potential, many of us can look at each of the nine types
and find our own personality relatively quickly.

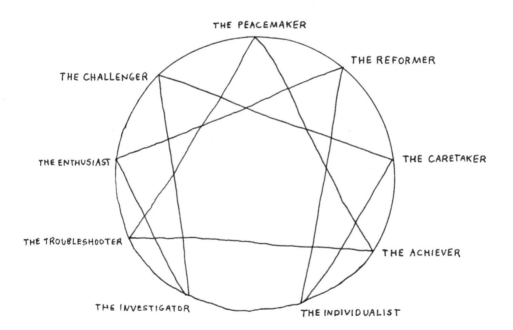

YOUR PERSONAL STORY

FIND YOUR TYPE

Read all nine descriptions in the pages that follow.

While one description might not feel exactly right in its entirety, note any sentences or phrases that resonate with you. There will likely be one personality type that resonates *most* with you.

Note also that within each type, personalities can range from functional to dysfunctional (or when traits are carried to extremes). To illustrate both the different personality types and the ranges within each, we are using characters from the story "Cinderella."

Find your type (or the two or three that resonate most) and gently observe over the course of a week the ways you reflect your particular personality type. Do you see yourself playing into any of the expectations? Do you behave a certain way when you want your needs to be met? What happens in moments when you feel more desperate to get something that you need?

ARE YOU A REFORMER?

ENNEAGRAM TYPE ONE

DO YOU FEEL PRESSURE TO DO THINGS PERFECTLY OR MAKE THINGS RIGHT?

ARE YOU EASILY FRUSTRATED OR ANNOYED WHEN THINGS AREN'T DONE JUST SO?

WHEN YOU WERE YOUNG, DID YOU WORRY ABOUT BEING PERFECT OR BEING A GOOD GIRL?

Reformers hold high ideals and standards. Because of this, they can be principled and responsible. When Reformers fixate on perfectionism, however, their attention automatically focuses on correcting errors and judging themselves and others.

THE "SHOULDS" OF A REFORMER

AN OVERLY FIXATED REFORMER

Cinderella inspires others to be good, serves justice, and never does anything wrong. She is a meticulous housekeeper.

Cinderella's stepmother is so fixated on perfection that she becomes harsh and tyrannical.

ARE YOU A CARETAKER?

ENNEAGRAM TYPE TWO

DO YOU FEEL THAT YOU ARE PRESSURED TO ALWAYS BE THERE FOR OTHERS?

DO YOU FEEL SAD THAT OTHERS DON'T RECOGNIZE THAT YOU HAVE NEEDS BUT EXPECT YOU TO BE THERE FOR EVERYONE ELSE?

AS A YOUNG GIRL, DID YOU FEEL LIKE YOU HAD TO ANTICIPATE EVERYONE ELSE'S NEEDS AND BE OF SERVICE TO THEM?

Caretakers are socially skilled, deeply attuned to others, and hardworking. Because of these gifts, they can be helpful and very generous. However, when Caretakers fixate on another's needs, they begin to create an unspoken, unconscious contract by which they expect to have their needs met in return. Caretakers may become resentful because their own needs aren't being met and may become driven to be indispensable, trying to become the ideal caregiver. In their most fixated state, Caretakers may begin to challenge boundaries by overdoing the "people-pleasing" and acting like martyrs.

THE "SHOULDS" OF A CARETAKER

AN OVERLY FIXATED CARETAKER

Cinderella is always there to serve. She anticipates other people's needs so effectively that she can provide for others before they even ask.

Cinderella's stepmother tries to make Cinderella feel guilty about everything she has "given" her. Playing a martyr, she tells Cinderella that she is helping her despite the girl's limitations and undesirability.

65

ARE YOU AN ACHIEVER?

ENNEAGRAM TYPE THREE

| DO YOU FEEL PRESSURED TO BE THE BEST AND MOST SUCCESSFUL? | DO YOU FIND THAT YOU JUDGE OTHERS WHO CAN'T SUCCEED? | AS A LITTLE GIRL, DID YOU FEEL LIKE YOU COULD NEVER LET YOURSELF FAIL? |

Achievers can be some of the most productive and effective people. Because of their gifts, Achievers are able to focus on tasks, goals, and "doing," all of which seems to be effortless for them. When Achievers become overly fixated on success, however, they start to feel pressured to win at all costs. If an Achiever's fixation is not satisfied, they may start to practice deception so they appear to be successful even when they're not.

| THE "SHOULDS" OF AN ACHIEVER | AN OVERLY FIXATED ACHIEVER |

Cinderella is admirably beautiful and efficient. And it's seemingly effortless, making her ability to achieve look easy.

The stepsisters are driven to achieve the prince's love despite all the odds, even keeping Cinderella away from the ball and, in one version of the story, cutting off their toes in an attempt to fit into the glass slipper.

"IN YOURSELF LIES
THE WHOLE WORLD
AND IF YOU KNOW
HOW TO LOOK AND
LEARN, THEN THE
DOOR IS THERE AND
THE KEY IS IN YOUR
HAND. NOBODY ON
EARTH CAN GIVE YOU
EITHER THAT KEY OR
THAT DOOR TO OPEN
EXCEPT YOURSELF."

KRISHNAMURTI
PHILOSOPHER / POET

ARE YOU AN INDIVIDUALIST?

ENNEAGRAM TYPE FOUR

DO YOU FEEL PRESSURED TO BE UNIQUE?

DO YOU ENVY OTHERS WHO STAND OUT OR WHO ARE ADMIRED?

AS A LITTLE GIRL, DID YOU FEEL LIKE YOU HAD TO BE SPECIAL OR UNIQUE?

Individualists show emotional depth, a commitment to truth, and are focused on being unique and different. Their gifts are authentic emotional expression and creativity that touches universal human experience. But when the Individualist's needs to be special and authentic are not being met, or when they are seized by fear of abandonment, they may resort to envy and recklessness, and may overact dramatically. At their worst, Individualists may withdraw from others, may become very entitled, and may lose their ability to relate in an emotionally appropriate way to other people.

THE "SHOULDS" OF AN INDIVIDUALIST

AN OVERLY FIXATED INDIVIDUALIST

Cinderella is a unique candidate to be chosen as a bride. Although she comes from a humble background, she seems to be authentic and worthy of a prince.

The stepmother and stepdaughters envy Cinderella because they think she is more beautiful than they are. They abandon social decency and mock Cinderella to make her feel badly in front of the prince.

ARE YOU AN INVESTIGATOR?

ENNEAGRAM TYPE FIVE

DO YOU FEEL PRESSURED TO HAVE THE MOST REASONABLE & BEST-RESEARCHED POINT OF VIEW?

DO YOU FEAR THAT OTHERS MIGHT COME INTO YOUR LIFE & DISRUPT YOUR CAREFULLY ORGANIZED PLANS?

DO YOU FEAR SOMEONE WHO MIGHT INVADE YOUR PRIVATE SPACE?

AS A LITTLE GIRL, DID YOU FEEL LIKE YOU HAD TO COMMUNICATE VERY SELECTIVELY— NOT SHARING FULLY THE INFORMATION YOU HAD?

Investigators are quick to notice information and identify intruders because they seek objectivity, privacy, and independence. They are deeply knowledgeable and appear calm in a crisis, because Investigators are driven by the need to analyze everything and not to let emotion cloud their judgment or expose their inner world. If this drive becomes obsessive, they may isolate themselves from others because closeness may weaken their stance.

THE "SHOULDS" OF AN INVESTIGATOR

AN OVERLY FIXATED INVESTIGATOR

Cinderella does not show her emotions or grief to the outside world and remains mostly observant so that she barely interacts with anyone.

Cinderella's stepmother acts miserly toward Cinderella and devises ways to keep her locked up so that Cinderella can't penetrate her safety zone.

ARE YOU A TROUBLESHOOTER?

ENNEAGRAM TYPE SIX

DO YOU FEEL PRESSURED TO CONSTANTLY SCAN THE ENVIRONMENT FOR POTENTIAL RISKS?

ARE YOU SUSPICIOUS OF OTHERS' MOTIVATIONS AND HOW THEY MIGHT IMPACT YOU AND THOSE YOU LOVE?

AS A LITTLE GIRL, DID YOU FEEL LIKE YOU HAD TO PROTECT YOUR FAMILY FROM THE DANGERS THAT YOU COULD SEE AROUND THEM?

Troubleshooters are naturally vigilant and attentive to signs of possible danger. They want to be aware of any potential hazards and seek security in the form of authority or a structure that they can follow. As a result, Troubleshooters are sensitive and loyal. When caught in fear, however, they cause others to feel insecure and on guard, disrupting people's sense of safety instead of being a source of strength and reliability. If not checked, the drive for safety overrides everything and becomes ineffective or difficult, and Troubleshooters become anxiety-ridden and, in extreme instances, paranoid.

THE "SHOULDS" OF A TROUBLESHOOTER

AN OVERLY FIXATED TROUBLESHOOTER

Cinderella is loyal without complaint while watching out for the safety of a few select others.

Reactionary and unpredictable, Cinderella's stepmother tries to incite fear in Cinderella and disrupt her sense of safety.

ARE YOU AN ENTHUSIAST?

ENNEAGRAM TYPE SEVEN

DO YOU FEEL PRESSURED TO FEEL GOOD ALL THE TIME AND TO HANG OUT WITH OTHER PEOPLE WHO FEEL SIMILARLY IN ORDER TO KEEP FEELING GOOD?

DO YOU FIND THAT YOU RUN FROM BOREDOM AND PAIN?

AS A LITTLE GIRL, DID YOU FEEL LIKE YOU HAD TO BE GOOD AT A LOT OF THINGS AND PUT ON A HAPPY FACE NO MATTER WHAT?

Enthusiasts love having the freedom to choose and explore many options. They are upbeat, positive, and energized, and offer their gifts of creative and multidisciplinary thinking to the world. When caught by fear, Enthusiasts may be driven to impulsively preserve their freedom by becoming extremely restless, scattered, and self-oriented. At their worst, Enthusiasts appear manic and narcissistic.

THE "SHOULDS" OF AN ENTHUSIAST

AN OVERLY FIXATED ENTHUSIAST

Cinderella is very playful and optimistic with her fairy godmother despite her unhappy life with her stepmother and stepsisters.

The stepsisters, who are purely self-oriented with an insatiable need to have their desires met by Cinderella, do not notice or care about the pain they are causing her.

ARE YOU A CHALLENGER?

ENNEAGRAM TYPE EIGHT

DO YOU FEEL
PRESSURED TO
DOMINATE SO
THAT NO ONE
CAN DOMINATE
YOU?

DO YOU USE
YOUR WILL TO
GET WHAT YOU
WANT?

AS A LITTLE GIRL, DID
YOU FEEL LIKE YOU
HAD TO BE STRONG TO
PROTECT YOURSELF
AND THOSE WHOM
YOU LOVED?

Challengers are driven by power or by appearing powerful and protective. They are assertive and dominate situations with their fearless presence. When feeling fearful, vulnerable, or out of control, Challengers may compensate by being overpowering and confrontational. In their most fixated state, Challengers may be repulsed by the vulnerability they see in others, triggering a dangerous reaction in which they may use their power to intimidate or harm others.

THE "SHOULDS" OF A CHALLENGER

AN OVERLY FIXATED CHALLENGER

Cinderella eventually becomes a magnanimous leader in charge of those who have been unjust to her.

The stepmother exerts her power over Cinderella, ordering her around, bullying her with threats, and making her stay home from the ball.

ARE YOU A PEACEMAKER?

ENNEAGRAM TYPE NINE

DO YOU FEEL PRESSURED TO BE SEEN AS NONCONFRONTATIONAL, COMPLIANT, AND EASY TO BE WITH?

DO YOU GET UNCOMFORTABLE WHEN YOU THINK ABOUT WHAT YOU LIKE OR NEED?

AS A LITTLE GIRL, DID YOU FEEL LIKE YOU COULD NOT ADMIT TO ANY NEEDS OF YOUR OWN FOR FEAR OF BEING A BOTHER?

Peacemakers are naturally inspired to create harmony and unity among people. They instinctively sense conflict and, in an easygoing way, can figure out what actions will allow others to function more cooperatively. Their unpretentious, down-to-earth presence makes it possible for others to relax. In extreme situations, Peacemakers may get stuck when they focus on blending in to such a degree that they lose themselves as individuals. They become frozen in inaction and disconnected from their anger at not being seen.

THE "SHOULDS" OF A PEACEMAKER

AN OVERLY FIXATED PEACEMAKER

Cinderella emanates love without causing waves or expressing her own needs.

One of the stepsisters becomes so fixated on not making waves that she becomes lazy, dependent on Cinderella to do everything.

ELLE:

THE ENTHUSIAST

When I was a kid, my mom would come into my room when it was time to go to bed. Often she would discover me sprawled across the floor, fascinated by a large, complicated art project that had taken over my bedroom. I would promise her that I was going to sleep soon, and she would go off to get ready for bed. In what seemed like only a minute, Mom was back at my door in her pajamas giving me The Look. "Just a few more minutes!" I would plead. She would go back to bed, but the art project was never finished, and it wasn't until hours later that I would collapse in exhaustion and haul myself to bed.

Fast-forward a few decades. I was in Atlanta for an event, and someone offered to pick me up at my hotel to escort me to the event. I was in my room, hurriedly trying to put the finishing touches on a watercolor when I realized I was going to be late. I bolted downstairs, arriving with a few minutes to spare, which was unusual for me. When the driver pulled up, I got in the car and he said with eyebrows raised, "You're on time. They told me you'd be late and gave me all of these ways to contact you." Next to my elbow on the center console was a piece of paper containing my hotel information, my phone number, and a few notes. I glanced at the page and read:

"Please note: Elle always runs late so plan accordingly . . ."

I stopped reading and started to go numb. When we arrived at the event, I tried my best to put on a happy face and forget about it. But later, once I was back in my hotel room, I thought about it again and asked myself, "Well, is it true?"

It was. I frequently ran late, bailed on commitments if something more enticing came up, and harbored the mentality that if I was having fun doing one thing, why would I stop to do something else?

When I learned about the Enneagram, I was fascinated. I realized that my path to growth would involve bringing awareness to this gluttony in my life. As I started to see this play out in real time, I understood that my actions impacted others, sometimes deeply.

As I thought about what motivated me to bail on my commitments, I realized it often came down to a fear of boredom. I discovered that it was common for Enthusiasts to organize their lives around having fun, or "staying high," in order to avoid the humdrum parts of life. It was as though life was a buffet, and I wanted to try *everything*.

A few months later, I stood in the shower and on the fogged-over glass shower door, I began to write with my index finger: B-O-R-I-N-G. I asked myself, *What does "boring" mean?* Without thinking, and with the stream of water putting me into a trancelike state, I began to write words like: dependable, reliable, committed . . .

With time and gentle awareness, I began to slow down, to practice saying "no" to projects, and to fully commit when I said yes. It turns out that focus brings immense depth and a relaxed feeling to my life, which feels good. Instead of feeling an inch deep and a mile wide, I now feel like I am running on a fuel that is deeper and more deliberate, and I channel this new kind of energy into choice commitments. With time, as I loosened my fixation on gluttony, I started to feel sure-footed, fulfilled, and joyful.

SUSIE :

THE PEACEMAKER.

I was judgmental about selfish people. People who put themselves first, who are really vocal about their needs and cause conflicts to get what they want, grated on my nerves. Selfish was not OK in my book so I devised a way to ensure *I* was never called selfish. I would show everyone I met how cooperative and easygoing I could be. I would defend other people and causes and stand up for the rights of others, but I wouldn't stand up for myself and tarnish my reputation as a giving and kind person.

This defense mechanism worked exquisitely until I needed something. I always felt wonderful when someone would say how easy it was to be around me, or how spiritual and unconditionally loving I was. It was a good gig. However, when I started to have health problems as a result of people smoking cigarettes around me, or when I found that eating certain foods caused stomachaches, I was challenged. It started to seem odd watching myself go through physical pain rather than make waves by saying, "Please don't smoke around me," or "I'm sorry, but I can't eat that lovely dish you have prepared."

It wasn't until I was in a graduate program in psychology that I got a window view into the absurdity of this ego stance. I was in a role-play where each person had to vote on who would get kicked off a fictional lifeboat. There were nine people but only room for eight, so someone needed to be sacrificed for the others to survive. I figured the polite thing to do was to vote myself off. Well, I was surprised to find that everyone else had voted me off as well (because everyone else had children). I was shocked. No one, not even I, looked out for my own life.

If I was so selfless, how could I be kicked off? It would be like kicking a kitten out of the boat. I was sure people would opt to keep me because I was so easygoing and loving. Not only had my defense not worked, but my offer to sacrifice myself meant just that. I would die.

It was then that I started to remember myself as a child, terrified of admitting I had needs, especially if it was a need that I didn't understand how to meet. I had somehow concluded that asking for help or insisting on having something I needed was contrary to my survival. I would put off doing things that were in my own best interest. As a nine-year-old, self-sacrifice was my go-to behavior, but it didn't work. My self-sacrificing was not done out of love, but out of fear and a need to be loved. I was so cooperative that I assumed others would look out for my needs. I would let others make decisions for me rather than voice my needs and risk upsetting others.

I had to learn that not only was it OK to act in my own self-interest, but that I had to be the one to look out for my survival. My friends and lovers were interested in helping but not in being responsible for me. They weren't interested in someone who did not state her preferences or stand up for herself. They were tired of the burden of guessing what I needed and trying to make sure I got it.

I have gradually learned to say what I think, take care of myself, and not sacrifice myself needlessly to the whims of others.

YOUR PERSONAL STORY

FOCUS YOUR STORY

On note cards, write down short versions of eight to ten stories you tell yourself about yourself. Have these stories changed over time? For Susie, she learned that part of her personal story was:

> I SHOULD ALWAYS TAKE CARE OF EVERYONE ELSE BEFORE MYSELF

Next, pin all of your cards up on a wall and look at them as a set.

As you look at the cards, start to look for patterns. Maybe part of your story is "I am good at accommodating difficult people (Personal Story) because I come from a family who is here to make positive change in the world (Family Story)." Or, "I've never been good at using my voice (Personal Story) because I learned from an early age not to rock the boat (Cultural Story)." Or, "I was loved as a girl (Family Story), but I have felt less loved as I have become an older woman (Cultural Story)."

Now, looking at your note-card wall and using the examples from Susie's and Elle's stories, what features of your survival strategies are no longer working in a positive way?

Do you see any parts that you would like to shift? Are there any aspects of your story that you want to come forward and play a larger role in your life? By using cards, you can see the significant beats of your life story—which otherwise would be sprawling and difficult to grasp—and study them.

For example, you may assess the difference between real fear and imagined fear. Or you may identify a behavior that has grown so strong that it has become fanatical and is actually causing the opposite of the intended effect. Susie experienced this when she realized her survival strategy was to be a Peacemaker, not making any waves and being invisible. Once she was able to see the effects of this story she had been telling herself about herself, she realized there was no way she could keep behaving that way, and she needed to change. She made it a goal to begin expressing her needs, in small ways at first, by saying, for example, where she wanted to go to dinner if she was in a group. As she got more comfortable, she focused on larger issues, such as telling her father how she wanted him to treat her.

Looking at your own cards, you can choose where you want your story to go next.

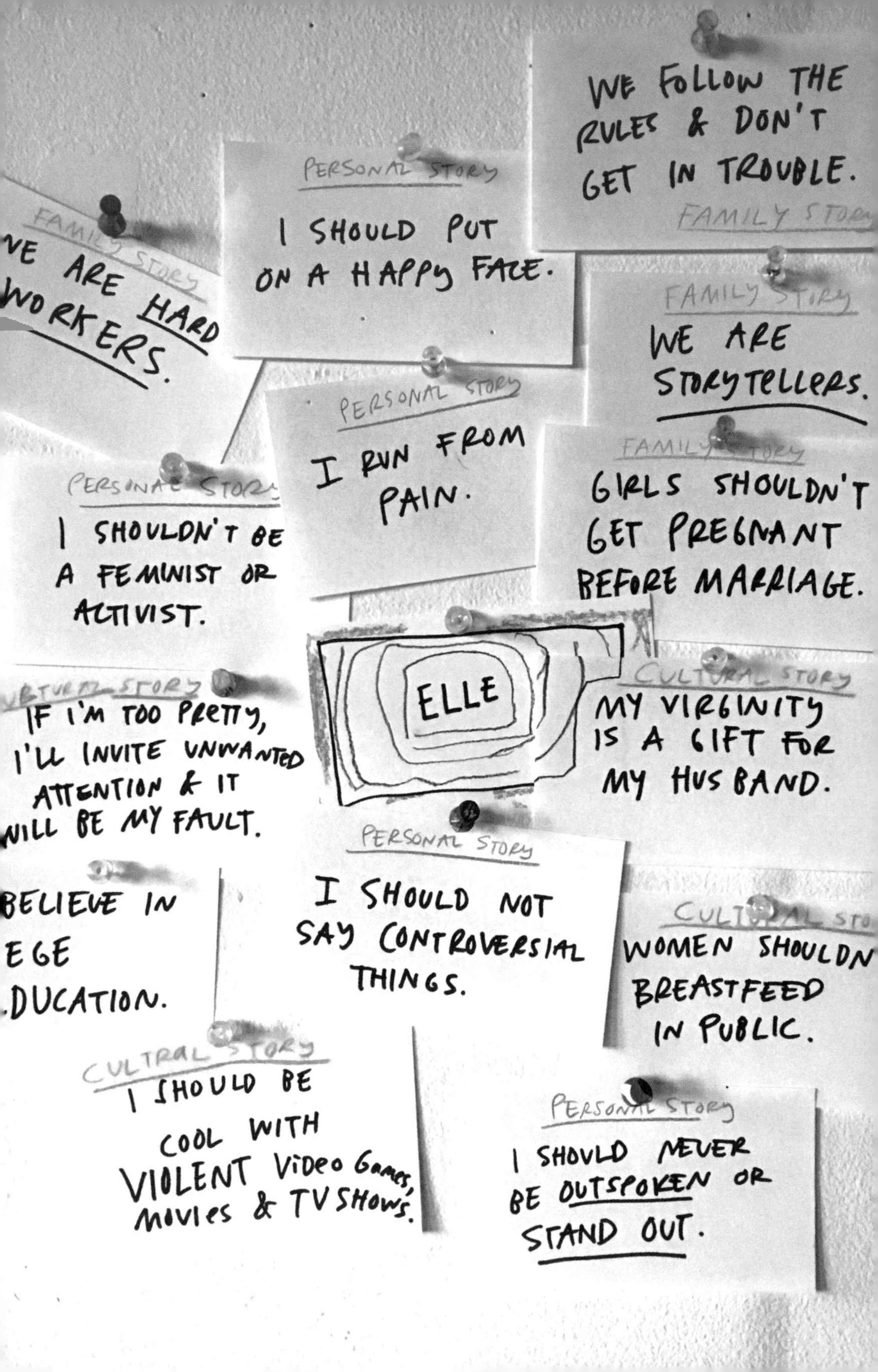

YOU NEED TO BE:
- KIND
- GIVING
- SELF-SACRIFICING

I CAN'T DISAPPOINT ANYBODY.

BE STRONG & DYNAMIC, BUT DO DO ANYTHING OUTS THE RULES.

WOMEN ARE THE PROBLEM.

THE HERRICKS ARE ENTERTAINERS & CHARISMATIC, BUT THEY DON'T ASK FOR ANYTHING.

WOMEN ARE GREAT AT HOSTIN PARTIES.

I SHOULD ALWAYS TAKE CARE OF OTHERS' NEEDS BEFORE MINE.

SUSIE

I AM CUTE LIKE A KITTEN, HOW COULD YOU WANT TO HURT ME?

BOYS ARE LOGICAL.

SUPPOSED TO THIN THAT I SIT DOWN THIGHS DON'T TOUCH.

YOU ARE HERE TO SAVE THE WORLD.

WOMEN ARE IRRATIONAL & HYSTERICAL.

S SHOULD E MORE RIVILEGES.

FAMILY STICKS TOGETHER.

I AM KIND & ARTISTIC AND NOT DETAIL-ORIENTED.

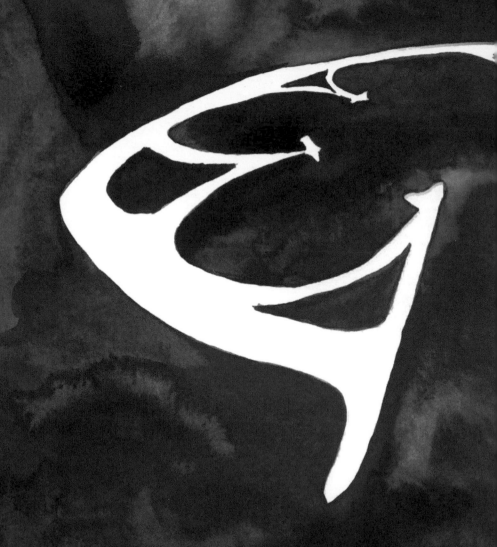

PART THREE

THE CENTER OF YOUR STORY

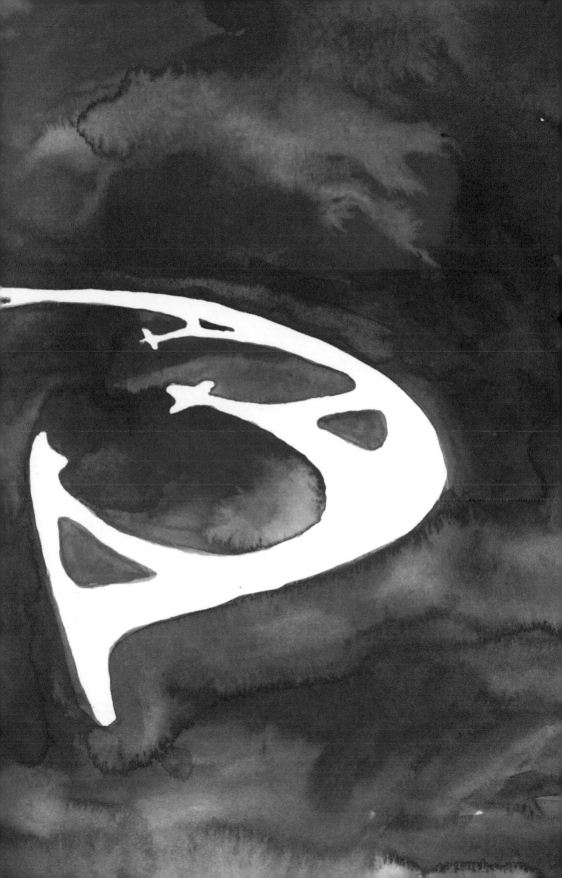

"THE LABYRINTH IS THOROUGHLY KNOWN. WE HAVE ONLY TO FOLLOW THE THREAD OF THE HERO PATH... AND WHERE WE HAD THOUGHT TO SLAY ANOTHER, WE SHALL SLAY OURSELVES. WHERE WE HAD THOUGHT TO TRAVEL OUTWARD, WE WILL COME TO THE CENTER OF OUR OWN EXISTENCE. AND WHERE WE HAD THOUGHT TO BE ALONE, WE WILL BE WITH ALL THE WORLD."

JOSEPH CAMPBELL
MYTHOLOGIST

You have seen how stories have affected you; you may have gained insight into internal structures of your mind that you inherited from your family or community; you may have seen how your ego built ways to keep you safe; and now, you are seeing how those same structures, stories, and strategies might actually be obsolete. This path is the meandering, spiraling journey toward the center of the labyrinth.

This work and its rewards tend to evolve over time, but the first steps are here.

The journey to the center of your story is, in a sense, the journey to the present moment. It can be helpful to learn to quiet what Buddhists call the "monkey mind," or "chattering mind."

IN THIS DEEP INNER-SILENCE, YOU MIGHT ENCOUNTER A HIGHER TRUTH OR PROFOUND VOICE FROM WITHIN.

"THE LABYRINTH IS A MIRROR OF THE SOUL."

KATE WOLF-PIZOR
PSYCHOTHERAPIST

At Chartres Cathedral in France, there is a labyrinth at the center of the church. Its design is unique; it looks like a flower with six petals, and the stem is the walkway both in and out. We see this as a metaphor or a reminder that there is only one way into yourself and one way out because you are the container of yourself. You are the only entrance to you. And it is here that you can be alone with yourself and enjoy the emptiness of the space. If you see others at the center inside of you, they are merely aspects of your history and the culture that has shaped you. Only you can be at the center of you.

Once you have identified some of the influences and forces in your life that have led you to be who you are, you can imagine a way of looking at the world through fresh eyes. Because you are now at the center, awake to the influences of the aspects of your psyche. Maybe you discovered that there are aspects of yourself that you desire to bring forward.

Imagine Cinderella walking the labyrinth. She's a woman who wants to change her life—in her situation, that means meeting a prince. Her stepmother's and stepsisters' complaints and directives are a metaphor for how the mind works. "You can't have this, you can't have that. . . And if you do . . . Then you should . . . " Imagine Cinderella finally getting to the center of the labyrinth, having let go of those voices, and exclaiming, "But I want to meet the prince!" And, as heroines do, even amidst her horrible situation, she uses the power of her imagination to visualize what she wants, and a plan emerges that will help her achieve her dream. In some versions of the story, Cinderella sits in her corner of the kitchen imagining a better life.

It is then that her fairy god(dess)mother, the symbol of that part of us that can think in new ways, comes forth. She waves a wand, and Cinderella gets all she needs to meet the prince. It seems as if this is all done by "magic" and is a temporary illusion, but there is the slipper that somehow remains material. In a sense, the slipper becomes the bridge between imagining and manifesting.

This is our dream for you—that you have access to your imagination to help you achieve what you want from life. As you enter into the heart of your story, here are some tips and tricks to help the process of transformation.

"In my own little corner
in my own little chair
I can be whatever
I want to be.
On the wings of my fancy
I can fly anywhere
and the world will open its arms
to me."

RODGERS AND HAMMERSTEIN,
CINDERELLA

YOU ARE IN CHARGE OF YOUR INTERNAL WORLD.

Call them your inner committee or your mind family—there are many voices that offer opinions or advice on your actions. In many spiritual traditions, becoming aware of these voices and then learning to separate from them is an important goal. When you recognize all of the different parts of yourself and hear each one, you begin to realize that you are separate from those voices. As you gradually become aware of all of your inner voices, the more you will be able to choose—in real time—how you want your story to unfold.

HONOR THE ASPECTS OF YOUR PERSONALITY THAT HAVE HELPED YOU TO SURVIVE SO FAR.

It's important to give credit where it's due. We have all developed aspects of our internal world that have simply been trying to keep us safe and protect us. For instance, the part of you that says, "Don't fall in love!" is a protective muscle. While we might want to relax these parts of ourselves, it's important to honor and thank the parts of you that did the best they could to protect you.

A Japanese martial art called Aikido exemplifies this practice. Aikido was developed to protect both the person being attacked and the attacker from injury. For example, if an attacker is running full speed at an Aikido practitioner, the person being attacked would try to both defend and redirect, or turn the energy back on the attacker and then quickly bring them to a place of rest so that no one gets hurt. You've probably seen an example of this if you've seen a martial arts scenario where the attacker appears to be effortlessly deflected and flipped into a prone position. Aikido emphasizes compassion for the well-being of the attacker. You can practice Aikido, in a way, by extending compassion to the parts of your internal world that have been "attacking" you.

FIRE, HIRE, OR RETRAIN ASPECTS OF YOURSELF

This might be the most powerful practice that you can use in your internal world. It will reward you for life if you put the effort into it. As you gently bring self-awareness to your inner voices and fixations, you will gain the capacity to fire, hire, or retrain those voices and fixations.

Your fixations, having been developed early in life in order to keep you safe, are fierce. They have been in charge for a reason, and that is exactly what makes this work difficult. Retraining old inner voices, giving them new tasks, or asking them to stop doing old things and start doing new things might feel threatening. You might even feel like a part of you is dying. But this is what's necessary for *you* to take control of your inner world and your story. You will see incredible change in your life if you stick with it.

When Susie began dealing with her inner misogynist, she would imagine that it was an inner voice sitting on her board of directors, and she would talk directly to it, as though it was real and present. First, she would give it credit, saying,

THANK YOU FOR HELPING ME TO SURVIVE SO FAR.

Then, she would say specifically how she wanted to retrain it, adding,

I NO LONGER WANT YOU TO REPORT TO ME IN A CRITICAL WAY.

Finally, she would tell this very real part of her what would happen if it didn't start to change its tune, saying,

IF YOU KEEP TALKING TO ME CRITICALLY, I WILL PRACTICE IGNORING YOU.

As you dialogue with your own inner voices, you will be able to listen as they retire their defenses and get in line, doing what *you* want them to do and helping *you* write the story that you want to be living.

"NO ONE IS BORN HATING ANOTHER PERSON BECAUSE OF THE COLOR OF THEIR SKIN, OR THEIR BACKGROUND, OR THEIR RELIGION. PEOPLE MUST LEARN TO HATE, AND IF THEY CAN LEARN TO HATE,

THEY CAN BE TAUGHT TO LOVE, FOR LOVE COMES MORE NATURALLY TO THE HUMAN HEART THAN ITS OPPOSITE. "

NELSON MANDELA
FORMER PRESIDENT OF SOUTH AFRICA

ASSIGN NEW TASKS

In your own inner world, every part of you wants to be a team player and stay on the field. This is important to remember: All the parts of yourself want to be a part of you; they just might need some training and counsel on how to do it.

ELLE :

I would speak with the different parts of myself in real time by bringing awareness to the internal dialogue in my head. One day, I was crossing the street in San Francisco when I saw another woman crossing the street toward me. In my head, I heard a voice—my inner misogynist—say something horrible about the woman based on her appearance. Right then and there, I remembered my practice of using the process of naming the voice and telling it to change its tune. I told my inner misogynist that it was not okay to talk that way, and that it needed to say something nice to the woman. At the moment that thought occurred, the woman sneezed, and I got to say, "Bless you."

WHEN YOU TAKE ONE STEP TOWARD THE GODS THE GODS TAKE TEN STEPS TOWARD YOU.

FIND A SPECIAL OBJECT

From the Holy Grail to the Glass Slipper, special objects have symbolized important journeys. What is yours? This object might be something that caught your eye as a child or something that you have held close to your heart. Maybe it is an object that you wish you could have had, like Dorothy's ruby slippers, or maybe it is a recurring image that always feels particularly potent for you.

For Elle, she began to have a recurring dream about a white room. It had tall white walls, warehouse windows, and a cement floor. Eventually, she began to look for this dream in real life, and one day she found it: a warehouse for rent in San Francisco's Dogpatch neighborhood. On her first night in the white room she had visualized in her dreams, she began to panic because she didn't understand why this dream had called to her. "Why am I here?" she asked, and the room replied, "It's time to paint." While she had painted all the time as a little girl and even into college, somewhere along the way she just got busy and forgot about it. Honoring this dream is what inspired Elle to return to her life-affirming practice of creating art.

Dreams, objects, and images have the power to transform your life. They bridge the world of imagination to the here and now, and they give us courage when we are trying something new and potentially uncomfortable. For Cinderella, she left her glass slipper at the ball, which did not disappear like the rest of her magical gear that her fairy god(dess)mother conjured for her. Then the prince showed up with it, still in material form. The slipper can be seen as the bridge between the imagined and real world.

SUSIE:

When I was in Mexico in my twenties, I fell in love with the images of conch shells on the ancient pyramids there. I've visualized them many times over the years for their beauty and lasting power. Years after Mexico, I was at Mount Everest base camp and had a vision that I was meant to help lead women to find their power. The voice, which I call the internal misogynist, told me that the vision was vain and narcissistic. Who was I to suppose I could do such a thing? I tucked the vision away in the back of my mind, but never forgot it. Years later, I was given a fossil of a version of a conch shell. It was from the Mount Everest base camp! And it is the Tibetan symbol of awakening! Its symbolism includes focusing on your welfare and that of others. It was as if I were being knocked on the head with a sign that what I was longing for was also trying to find me so I could realize my vision. That was when I began to more consciously speak my mind. By doing that, I began to put myself in a position where people started asking me my opinions and eventually to take on leadership positions.

As you continue gently bringing self-awareness to your inner world, you are already beginning to take the story back from the storytellers, both real and imagined. And you get to decide what happens next. When you feel you can help choose the direction of your story, or how you feel about your story, joy starts to seep in, allowing for optimism and mirth to become your travel partners as you venture forth.

"THE DIFFERENCE BETWEEN A COMEDY AND A TRAGEDY IS THAT IN COMEDY THE CHARACTERS FIGURE OUT REALITY IN TIME TO DO SOMETHING ABOUT IT."

BENNETT W. GOODSPEED
ECONOMIC ADVISOR

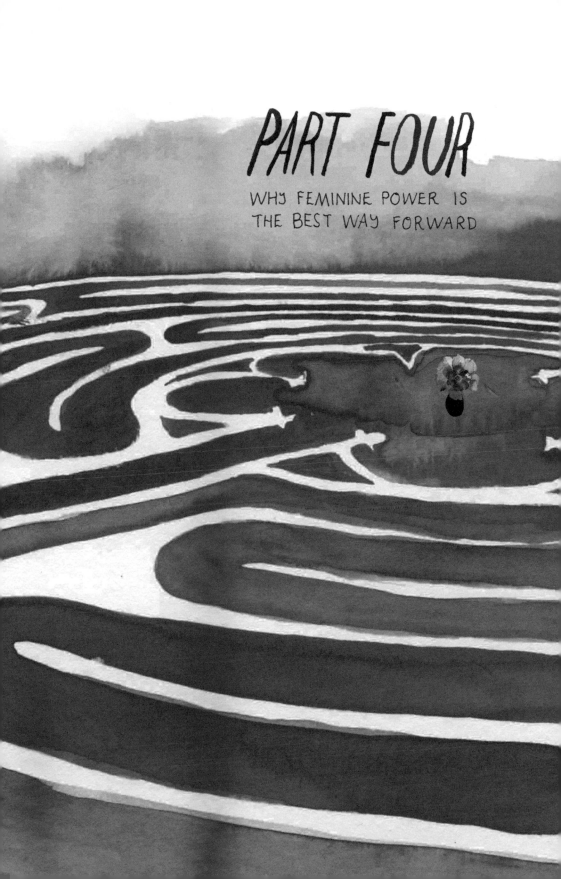

PART FOUR

WHY FEMININE POWER IS THE BEST WAY FORWARD

"THROW YOUR DREAMS INTO SPACE LIKE A KITE, AND YOU DO NOT KNOW WHAT IT WILL BRING BACK, A NEW LIFE, A NEW FRIEND, A NEW LOVE, A NEW COUNTRY."

ANAÏS NIN
AUTHOR AND ESSAYIST

Have you ever had a moment when things seemed totally aligned and exactly as they should be? Artists and writers often call this an epiphany, saying that the lyrics to a song simply "arrived" without any effort, as though from a place beyond themselves. It has also been called a "runner's high" or an endorphin rush, which is a fleeting surge of positive energy. Can you recall a time when you felt that everything was aligned and at peace in your life? Maybe it was a moment where you had utter certainty—even if it was about a difficult thing—or a feeling that everything was going to be okay, or maybe you felt at peace and confident in the future.

As women, seekers, and authors, we've gone through all of the steps in this book—and many more—over time. As we recognized and confronted our own internalized misogyny, the experience rippled through our lives and a beautiful feeling arose—a feeling of having come home.

SUSIE:

When I started to firmly handle and control my inner misogynist, I had boundless energy; I felt like I could do anything because I could imagine anything. I connected to the vitality of my own youth and the vitality of a full life before me. The world became a place to play and to learn because I felt unshackled. I could do what I wanted to do because the voices inside of me were now under my direction. I could still ask for their counsel, but for the most part, I had become my own captain, my own queen, my own longed-for friend and confidant. It was like finally getting a vitamin that had been denied.

ELLE:

After I identified the ways I was blocking myself as a woman, I had a dream. I was on an elevator in a floor-length red ball gown. Its long silky fabric flowed like waves around my legs. I took the elevator up to the very top floor. I stepped out into what looked like a sea of cubicles. The overhead lights were white, and the geometric shapes extended as far as I could see in every direction. All at once, I began running down the aisles, singing at the top of my lungs, and spinning and twirling in my red dress. When I woke up, I was shocked. I realized that it was the first time in my life I had ever had a dream where I had a voice—my feminine voice.

Power can be used to describe the effort used when exerting physical strength or authority over another person, or it can be used to describe someone's influence. But it can also be used to describe a person's electricity or energy. And in a woman, when her natural personality is freed from the confinement of a patriarchal system, a kind of generative energy is unleashed—this is what we call *Feminine Power*. Our friend Zandra Kaufman describes this phenomenon, saying,

"THE REASON IT IS GENERATIVE IS
THAT IT IS A POWER THAT IS NOT
EXERTED OVER ANOTHER BUT IS
A POWER THAT IS <u>WITH</u> ANOTHER."

Feminine Power is powerful because it is shared.

In India this power is personified in the goddess Devi. She is the creator of life and represents the fundamental reality of the universe— the creative source and the ultimate truth.

"I permeate the
earth and heaven,
all created entities
with my greatness,
and dwell in
them as eternal
and infinite
consciousness."

FROM THE DEVI SUKTA

"FEMININE POWER ISN'T SOMETHING WE GO OUT AND ACQUIRE; IT'S ALREADY WITHIN US.

IT'S **SOMETHING** THAT WE BECOME **WILLING TO** EXPERIENCE. SOMETHING TO ADMIT WE HAVE. "

MARIANNE WILLIAMSON
SPIRITUAL TEACHER

As you resolve the conflicts that stand between your defense systems and what is at the heart of your soul's longing, you will experience the infectious, generative, and inspiring power of being a free woman who is fully alive.

Like working your way through the labyrinth, the journey takes time. Sometimes you might feel like you are meandering back to where you started or that you are returning to the same place again and again. Even once you have reached the center of your story, it still takes time to continue to practice the lessons in this book. But as you continue to walk this meandering, twisting, and turning path, share feminine love with *yourself* and remember that small daily steps eventually lead to big leaps.

"HOW MIGHT WAR
AND CAPITALISM AND
CRIMINAL JUSTICE
AND A THOUSAND
OTHER THINGS
BE DIFFERENT HAD
THEY NOT BEEN DESIGNED
WITH HALF OF HUMANITY
LOCKED OUTSIDE THE DOOR?"

ANAND GIRIDHARADAS
AUTHOR

In science it is well established that for any ecosystem to survive, each of its diverse parts has to contribute uniquely as well cooperatively. If the contributions aren't balanced, or one aspect is consistently suppressed by another, then that system becomes fragile, incapable of change, and eventually dies. Sound familiar? The immense challenges that we face globally are because of the loss of the feminine. But we believe that women will bring about seismic shifts as the courage to bring our feminine voices forward grows. As you continue doing this work, remember that your strengths and gifts as a woman are real, and the global ecosystem needs them more than ever.

"BOTH NATURE AND NURTURE APPEAR TO HAVE SHAPED WOMEN INTO RELATIONAL EXPERTS."

MICHELE L. TAKEI
PSYCHOLOGIST

DISTINCT BRAIN FUNCTIONING

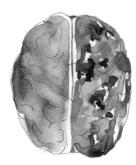

- *Women have more connections between the right and left hemispheres, which means: Women can retrieve information from different sides of the brain simultaneously, affecting what is called intuitive thinking, or making effective decisions quickly. Furthermore, having simultaneous access to the right brain, which is associated with creativity or imagination, indicates that women can be more readily compassionate and can more easily connect to the present moment.*

- *Women have more gray matter in the hippocampus, which means more neural density in this area.*

- *Women have very good working memory and process more emotional information and input from the senses.*

- *Women have more "wiring" in the area of the brain called the left caudate, which has been associated with social cognition. This means: Women tend to have good communication skills.*

- *Women have a greater density of mirror neurons, which means: Women are more comfortable with relationships because they can empathize with the emotional experiences of others.*

- *Women release oxytocin in times of stress, which means: Women have a tendency, under stress, to care for and befriend, which allows them to work in solidarity and to form communities rather than compete for resources.*

THE OPTION OF NONVIOLENCE

On average, 86 percent of violent crimes are committed by men.

"IF BY STRENGTH IS MEANT BRUTE STRENGTH, THEN, INDEED IS WOMAN LESS BRUTE THAN MAN. IF BY STRENGTH IS MEANT MORAL POWER THEN WOMAN IS IMMEASURABLY MAN'S SUPERIOR.... IF NONVIOLENCE IS THE LAW OF OUR BEING, THE FUTURE IS WITH WOMAN."

GANDHI

A TENDENCY TOWARD THE ALTRUISTIC

A group of Yale University researchers conducted twenty-two studies on altruism and discovered that women tend to be more altruistic than men. In the studies, they found that even women who identify themselves as having more traditionally "masculine traits" still exhibited greater generosity than men.

In 2006, Muhammad Yunus and his Grameen Bank were awarded the Nobel Peace Prize for their revolutionary social development work using microloans. Ninety-seven percent of the small loans were made to poor women in third-world countries. He saw that when he gave women small amounts of capital, they did not spend the money on alcohol or gambling, as the men did. Instead, they started or improved small businesses, improved the diets of their village's malnourished children, and sent kids to school. Their repayment track record is close to 97 percent, year after year. The lenders discovered that women who receive loans not only build successful businesses, but lead healthier lives and improve the lives of those around them.

It turns out that when we invest in women, women, in turn, invest in everyone.

AN ABILITY TO CREATE BEAUTY FOR HEALING PURPOSES

When a woman is pregnant, she often feels an urge to nest, adorning the space around her for her new baby. There is something powerful about creating a beautiful environment: A space that feels good, looks good, and smells good is a natural way to support a growing child and enhance our own well-being. Experiencing nature is another way to generate positive feelings. Being in beautiful settings is often a prescription for stress reduction. This makes sense because one definition of beauty is "something that pleasurably exalts the mind." Women seem to know this instinctively and, as a result, tend to create nurturing environments. It's also why so many women are stepping forward to protect the natural world.

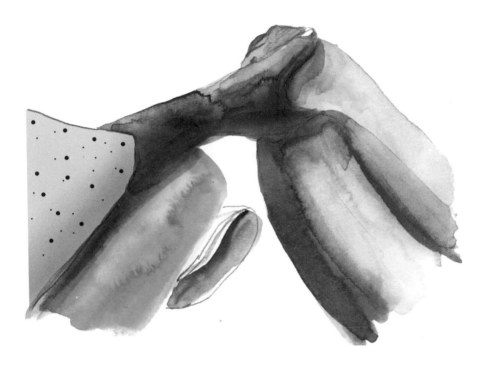

THE POWER TO TEND TO OTHERS WHEN UNDER STRESS

Women under stress produce the hormone oxytocin. This hormone creates a tendency to nurture others, which in turn decreases stress. You will actually feel a reduction in stress if you reach out to care for someone. This explains why, generally, in stressful situations, women seek to make contact with others. This innate behavior might be one of the reasons for women's naturally longer life span, i.e., community vs. life-shortening isolation.

THE ABILITY TO BEFRIEND IN ORDER TO SOLVE

Another side effect of oxytocin is the tendency to befriend others and collect in communities. The physicist David Bohm calls this cultivating "collective intelligence." He observed that when people were brought together to share and listen to one another in community dialogue, the ability to solve problems and implement change increased dramatically, as opposed to a more individualistic "every man for himself" approach of harboring intelligence for fear of competition.

THE EXPERIENCE OF FEMININE POWER
IS EXTRAORDINARILY HEALING, EVEN FOR MEN.

"I HAD THIS EXPERIENCE OF WHAT,
MEDICALLY, THEY CALL A STROKE, AND IT
WAS A DEATH IN THE MIND. SUDDENLY, A
TERRIFIC FORCE HIT ME AND THE MIND WENT!
EVERYTHING WENT!... PEOPLE THOUGHT I
WAS GOING TO DIE, AND I THOUGHT I WAS
GOING TO DIE... I SAID THE PROPER PRAYERS...
AND THEN I FELT A NEED TO SURRENDER....
IT CAME VERY CLEARLY, 'SURRENDER TO
THE MOTHER.' AND I MADE THIS ACT OF
SURRENDER AND A KIND OF WAVE OF LOVE
OVERWHELMED ME. THERE WAS A FRIEND,
A NURSE ... LOOKING AFTER ME, AND I
CALLED OUT TO HER AND SAID,

'I'VE BEEN OVERWHELMED
WITH LOVE! I DON'T KNOW
WHETHER I CAN SURVIVE IT!'

"IT WAS TREMENDOUS. THE FEMININE
SUDDENLY OPENED UP. BUT THAT WAS A
REAL DEATH, YOU SEE, OF THE MIND. AND
FROM THAT MOMENT ONWARDS, I HAVE
NEVER REALLY BEEN IN THE DUALISTIC
MIND. SOMETHING IS ALWAYS BEYOND IT."

FATHER BEDE GRIFFITHS
PRIEST

A CREATIVE VISION OF THE FUTURE

What if women could wake up to their skills and use them to bring about a world with more compassion, less violence, less hunger, led by both men and women? What would that world look like?

Many artists and writers, especially science fiction writers, have attempted to visualize this very thing.

Joan Slonczewski, a microbiologist and science fiction writer, poses a vision of a culture built on sharing and cooperation, showing the possibilities of true Feminine Power. Science fiction writer Ursula K. Le Guin depicts a society in which there is equality between the sexes in her novel *The Dispossessed*. Renaissance painter Ambrogio Lorenzetti used his talents to create images of a future with a strong female presence in his colorful, visionary mural *The Allegory of Good and Bad Government*. Hundreds of years later, this painting inspired the director of the American Civil Liberties Union, Anthony D. Romero, to file the first lawsuit against Donald Trump's "Muslim ban."

Gene Roddenberry, the creator of the original *Star Trek* television series, presented a future world where there is equality between the sexes as well as among the races. In a decision that would have profound implications, Roddenberry cast Nichelle Nichols, an African American woman, in the role of Lt. Nyota Uhura, one of the key officers on the USS *Enterprise*. At a time when television roles for African Americans were rare, seeing Nichols in this role would have a profound impact on many, including a young girl who happened to be watching.

"Well, when I was nine years old, Star Trek came on. I looked at it and I went screaming through the house, 'Come here, Mom, everybody, come quick, come quick, there's a black lady on television and she ain't no maid!' I knew right then and there I could be anything I wanted to be."

WHOOPI GOLDBERG
ACTRESS

In Part Two we talked about how the Enneagram is a tool that you can use to watch how personality stops you from getting to the center of your story; how our personal myths and go-to behaviors become our way of survival and thus become addictive. This becomes a vice that is so indelibly etched in our minds that change appears scary. Like internal patriarchy, the warning signals from these patterns keep us at bay from parts of ourselves that we long for.

"Optimism is the faith that leads to achievement."

HELEN KELLER
AUTHOR AND ACTIVIST

Because we are all different and have different challenges that keep us from our sense of possibility, our agency, it's the vision of what we can achieve that lights the caverns of despair. When the block is cleared, our newly found internal director can see where to go. In Whoopi's case she saw a woman in a role that was not defined by race—a vision with a dissolved obstacle. Because of this, Whoopi got the courage to pursue her dream, and we got to receive her gifts to the world—her inspiring and invigorating approach to humor, acting, and, most of all, her activism. Gene Roddenberry posed a vision and Whoopi leapt.

When you realize what lies within the terrain of the dream, then jumping into that terrain seems brave and attainable. In the Enneagram, this is sometimes called the passion-to-virtue leap. You leap from a behavior driven by passion, which can be compulsive, to an action of virtue that brings you closer to your dream—which in turn is fueled by your personality type. These parts all work in coordination with one another. Like the conversation with the internal misogynist, to go against the compulsion can feel dangerous, but when you leap, it is invigorating. The energy that results is the essence of Feminine Power. It will bring the authentic *you* into the world.

This is an emotional transformation. Rejection of parts of yourself is what keeps you in the loop of your vice. Self-compassion, created by getting to the center of your story, gives you courage to make the leap inspired by your dream. If you experience love for yourself in your heart, you can't help do what is best for that heart.

In the descriptions below, we use the term *passion/vice* to identify a behavior based on a compulsion to act to make a wounded heart feel better. The term *virtue* is used to convey the result of the reclaimed or healed heart.

PASSION/VICE ⟶ VIRTUE

THE REFORMER

ENNEAGRAM TYPE ONE

| PASSION/VICE | $\longrightarrow$ | VIRTUE |

ANGER

Resentment at the world's loss of goodness and feeling pressure to make it right.

SERENITY

The ability to realize and experience basic goodness for the perfection it is.

When Reformers bring gentle self-awareness to their personality structure, the pressure to reform begins to relax and they can begin to enjoy life as it is—perfectly imperfect.

When a Reformer goes to the center of her story, she experiences a release from her perceived rules because she can see how they were formed. She begins to see that she has been following a formula to be good, but the formula isn't getting her to her goal because she does not feel good. At the center of her story is the longing to be good, and she realizes she is innately good and sacred that nothing needs to be changed. Her resentment about not being able to fix the world dissipates and is replaced with a sense of serenity.

Her Feminine Power emerges because she knows that she is good and her serene sense of self-esteem inspires others to transform.

"THEY MUST FIRST LEARN TO VALUE THEIR OWN FEMININE QUALITIES,
AN INHERENTLY SPIRITUAL PROCESS, THEN EXORCISE
THEIR GUILT, ONE DAY AT A TIME — ONE TOXIC THOUGHT AT A
TIME — TO GET AT WHAT IS TRUE FOR THEM."

MICHELE L. TAKEI
PSYCHOLOGIST

THE CARETAKER

ENNEAGRAM TYPE TWO

PASSION/VICE   →   VIRTUE

PRIDE   HUMILITY

Pride at being the one who is focused on others. "I am better than others because I know how to take care of others."

Humility in realizing that there is no hierarchy and my needs are just as important as others' needs.

As Caretakers become aware of their personality structure, they begin to understand that their heart includes themselves; they see that they are loved and can release their obsession to fulfill the needs of others in order to get love.

When a Caretaker goes to the center of her story, she finds a love that is so vibrant and fulfilling that she ceases to be afraid that she is unloved. She falls in love with the girl in the story. She discovers that it was her fear that told her that she was unwanted and needed to be "the giving one." She realizes that she can feel the humility of having needs, as others do.

She regains the Feminine Power of humility by feeling connected to the abundant love from within, seeing herself as equally deserving as others.

THE ACHIEVER

ENNEAGRAM TYPE THREE

PASSION/VICE $\longrightarrow$ VIRTUE

DECEIT   VERACITY

To achieve at the cost of her own truth.

Expressing the true self, rather than one's image, becomes acceptable and appealing.

As Achievers grow in awareness of their personality, they will begin to see how their need to be seen as the successful one in order to prove their value has disconnected them from the intimacy and joy of their authentic self. They start to identify and express the truth even if they fear "looking bad."

When an Achiever reconnects to her heart, when her story demonstrates to her that her internal experience is fantastic, the fear that she has no value lessens. She experiences the preciousness of her own depth, and she feels connected to herself and to others. She experiences the virtue of her own truth, and can in turn share that truth with the world. The achiever models the facet of Feminine Power that is experiencing and expressing the precious truth with heart. With it comes a generous and humble kindness towards self and the world.

THE INDIVIDUALIST

ENNEAGRAM TYPE FOUR

PASSION/VICE	$\longrightarrow$	VIRTUE

ENVY

EQUANIMITY

Conveys sadness to show absence of significant purpose and to combat desperate fears of inadequacy in comparison to others.

With the experience of the self as truly unique, ordinary life ceases to feel dull or dangerous and one feels emotional balance.

As Individualists become more self-aware, they start to let go of their fear of being fundamentally flawed and begin to experience the calm sense of being deeply connected to everyone else. In the center of her story, an Individualist is able to connect to her sense of beauty, depth, and significance. When she accepts that she is truly unique, she gains room for others' uniqueness and relaxes in her own worthiness to live in a state equanimity.

THE INVESTIGATOR

ENNEAGRAM TYPE FIVE

PASSION/VICE	$\longrightarrow$	VIRTUE

AVARICE

NON-ATTACHMENT

Grasping at evidence and "proof" to make one feel safe and to allow for time to privately pursue reality through intellect.

Reconnecting to the intelligence of the heart and emotions reduces fear and releases attachment to seemingly objective data.

As Investigators grow, they start to relax their need to collect more and more information and begin to feel confident and secure in the world. They connect to the safety and support of a quieter, more relaxed mind, wherein they feel connected to and trust the innate intelligence of the universe.

When an Investigator enters into the center of herself, she experiences the loving presence of her true nature, and she releases the need to hoard information or other resources in order to feel protected. Relaxing into her Feminine Power, she lets go of the need to know everything and instead trusts her internal connection to love as a template to do the very thing she craves: to reach out to others.

"KNOWING WHAT MUST BE DONE DOES AWAY WITH FEAR."
ROSA PARKS

THE TROUBLESHOOTER

ENNEAGRAM TYPE SIX

PASSION/VICE	$\longrightarrow$	VIRTUE
FEAR		COURAGE

Mimics valor by presenting a doubting mind and a dependency on rules and authority.

Reconnection to the heart builds trust in self and others, replacing fear with hope.

As Troubleshooters grow in awareness and rely less on worry as a form of protection, their suspicions and fearfulness relax, and they are able to reconnect to their heart, accessing both love and courage. They practice their intuitive capacity to spot actual danger effortlessly.

When a Troubleshooter sees who is at the center of her story, she is able to relax because she sees that she is there to take the lead. Her inner guidance becomes her support system, and her heart becomes her touchstone so that she can release any sense of panic. Stepping out from the prison of the worried mind into the Feminine Power of trust in her intuition, the Troubleshooter revels in the courage that arises in her.

THE ENTHUSIAST

ENNEAGRAM TYPE SEVEN

PASSION/VICE	⟶	VIRTUE
GLUTTONY		SOBRIETY

Intense focus on ways to rapidly consume experiences in order to keep the fears of suffering and boredom at bay.

Accepting the reality and nature of emotional pain reduces the need for outside stimulus and brings about an internal sense of fulfillment.

As Enthusiasts bring gentle awareness to their need to keep moving on to new things, and as they slow down and take in the moment, they begin to feel a natural rising joy and feel satisfaction with what they have.

When an Enthusiast experiences the feast inside of her, her heart starts to feel fed. The original disconnect from the bountiful feeling of joy starts to heal, for at the center of her story she sees that she is interesting and lovable in all of her painful adventures. Her sense of emptiness and the terrors of being trapped in pain dissipate. The need to overindulge is replaced by a deep sense of sobriety, a pure joy that the inner life is truly abundant. The Enthusiast exudes the Feminine Power of love of the ordinary, comfortable self-restraint, and fulfillment in all aspects of existence.

THE CHALLENGER

ENNEAGRAM TYPE EIGHT

PASSION/VICE	→	VIRTUE
LUST		INNOCENCE

Attempts to control the environment and others by increasing intensity of interactions in order to avoid feeling weak and unwanted.

Accepting vulnerability dissipates the need to control, providng an intimate give-and-take relationship with others.

Challengers grow when they begin to share power and realize that real strength lies in their ability to be emotionally vulnerable to others.

When a Challenger connects to the center of her story, she sees the lost child of herself that learned she must toughen herself to survive. She feels a connection, and a longing, to touch that state of innocence. When she lets go, her vulnerability provides her with the strength she has wished for, and she no longer needs to protect herself through forcefulness. The Challenger's vulnerability enables her to connect with a profound sense of childlike openness, so she can truly believe she is wanted because she wants even the weakest part of herself, the child within.

The Challenger's Feminine Power is magnanimity because she accepts and loves her vulnerability.

THE PEACEMAKER

ENNEAGRAM TYPE NINE

PASSION/VICE $\longrightarrow$ VIRTUE

LAZINESS

CONSCIOUS ACTION

Seeks comfort in a distorted sense of love by merely not offending, sacrificing her needs in order to accommodate the needs of others.

The ability to take action despite the commotion it might cause, the self-sufficiency to pursue reconnecting to the self and pursuing one's needs and dreams.

When Peacemakers stop seeking harmony at all costs, they start to express their needs, overriding the fear of conflict, giving them energy to discern their own unique desires and needs.

When a Peacemaker arrives at the heart of her story, a deep sense of self-love arises. She accepts the drama and the waves she has created in her life because she is alive in her own story and is the star of her experiences. She no longer feels that she must remain invisible to be safe and discovers that true safety arises when she is in heartfelt connection with herself and what she cares about.

The Feminine Power of the Peacemaker is the ability to transcend the word *can't* and to take action for the benefit of self and others.

ACCESS YOUR FEMININE VOICE

TAKE YOUR DREAMS SERIOUSLY

If you want to learn more about your subconscious and unconscious desires, study your dreams. They are a powerful tool for accessing the hidden aspects of your mind. In dreams, you will find rich symbols, which you can interpret.

Because memories of your dreams will fade quickly, keep a pad of paper, journal, or recording device next to your bed or with you during the day in case you remember something about the dream. When a dream arises, record it immediately. Write down the essential parts of the dream, as well as colors, textures, and the way different experiences in the course of the dream made you feel. As you would in a recorded movie, pause your dream, look around at what you see, and try to clarify how you feel about it. The more you document about the dream, the more content you will have to delve deeper into the symbols and what they might mean for you.

Once you've written down your dream description, go through it and circle each item that might be a symbol for something else. Next to each symbol, write down what it means to you. After you write down your own meaning, you might want to research the symbol to find out what it means within your culture, although you can look at other cultures as well for ideas. Your night dreams are often very potent with symbols that seem very enigmatic at first, but the more you dig, the more you will discover.

You can use this same process for daydreams as well. For example, let's say that one day you start thinking of owls for no specific reason. You can ask yourself, "What do owls mean to me? What meaning does my culture attach to owls?" Your answers to those two questions might give you a clue about what's going on in your mind.

SUSIE :

I have a fear of spiders. They show up in my dreams consistently, which is quite frightening. In the psychology of Carl Jung, that means that I am afraid of that part of me that is represented by a spider.

I thought that spiders symbolized negative aspects of the feminine until I started researching other cultural references. The Navajo culture's Spider Woman was known for saving humans from monsters and enemies and taught them the art of weaving on a loom. In the Lakota tradition, spiderwebs catch dreams. According to Choctaw mythology, a grandmother spider stole fire from the people in the east for her people and safely carried it back to them. She bears the design on her torso to show her bravery. In the Hopi tradition, Spider Woman is the goddess of the earth and sang everything into worldly existence. In other Pueblo cultures, Spider Woman threw her dew-laced web across the sky, and the dew transformed into stars.

I realized that, for me, the spider represents my intimidating feminine side. I have been afraid to be powerful or intimidating, yet at the same time I longed for it. As a teenager, I was not in love with Captain Kirk or King Arthur, I wanted their jobs. I wanted to cultivate my own feminine leadership abilities—to let my power create a world I dreamed about. The spider was in my dreams to draw out the leader in me.

ELLE:

I have recurring dreams about snakes. In one of the earliest dreams, two snakes are swirling around my arms. One is fluorescent pink and the other is sapphire blue. Suddenly, one of the snakes bites one wrist, and then the other snake bites my other wrist, but the bites don't hurt. When these dreams started, I recorded them on my phone the moment I awoke.

Even though snakes in real life are quite scary, they were not scary in my dream. They felt like helpers or special guides, and their painless bites filled me with a warmth that felt like courage or inner fortitude.

I began to research snakes and discovered that they are ancient symbols for transformation because a snake is able to shed its dead skin while remaining alive, like a rebirth. The snake represents the *giver* of life. This dream was incredibly powerful because in my waking life at that time, whenever I would take a new step or try out a new skill, it would feel like parts of me were dying at the same time that all of this new growth was happening. Like the snake, I was shedding parts of myself.

I also learned that snakes were associated with the Egyptian goddess Wadjet, or Ua Zit, who was often represented as a cobra, and that women would use the venom from snakes as a tool for heightened awareness and prophecy. A few weeks later, I saw a video of a modern-day Burmese snake priestess who called a king cobra out of his den and kissed him—in spite of his hissing and agitated state—three times on his head in order to bring rain to her people. I was stunned not only because I had never seen someone kiss a king cobra but also because it was a snake *priestess*. I could not recall seeing many female spiritual leaders during my lifetime. It helped me see that divinity can be feminine just as it can be masculine.

A few months later, while traveling in Indonesia, I visited the home of a local family to take part in the sacred ancient water purification ceremony. The home smelled of sandalwood and jasmine, and it had a large family temple in which we gathered. At the front of the temple was an altar, and as I looked up at it, I saw a large statue of a Snake Goddess with thirteen cobras coming out of her head. And then a woman emerged and took her place at the altar. She was a snake priestess—a living, breathing Snake Goddess who was going to bless me with water.

The cobra continues to show up in my dreams, and whenever she arrives, I know that I am experiencing my own positive power as a woman to affirm life.

EXPLORE YOUR SENSES

If you feel that you may have lost touch with parts of your body over the years, kinesthetic experiences (learning with your body) can help awaken and enliven you.

- *Take a dance class centered on moving your hips, like Hula or Hip-Hop.*

- *Awaken your senses by exploring scents, using aromatherapy, kitchen spices, or candles.*

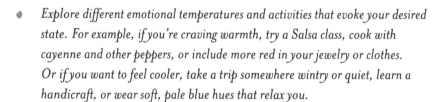

- *Explore different emotional temperatures and activities that evoke your desired state. For example, if you're craving warmth, try a Salsa class, cook with cayenne and other peppers, or include more red in your jewelry or clothes. Or if you want to feel cooler, take a trip somewhere wintry or quiet, learn a handicraft, or wear soft, pale blue hues that relax you.*

- *Become more aware of your body and the signals it's sending throughout the day: What can you taste, touch, smell, see, and hear right now?*

WRITE YOUR DEFINITION OF FEMININE POWER AND FIND A SYMBOL FOR IT

Writer Natasha Dern describes Feminine Power as " . . . [a] type of Mystical Radiance [that] permeates and radiates from women who are anchored within their body."

SUSIE'S SYMBOL OF FEMININE POWER

Many years ago, I found myself drawing red lotuses over and over again. I doodled them on notepads, made pastel drawings of them, and finally made one into a logo for a business. I loved the strength and beauty of them, and I knew lotuses were a symbol of the process of enlightenment. The mind evolves like the journey of the lotus as it grows from a seedling through the mud and water eventually to bloom in the sunlight; the water, the mud, and the sunlight represent the levels of consciousness. I knew I valued lotuses for the many things they represented to me, but why was I compelled to fill their petals with a fiery red?

I discovered that in Tibetan yoga dreaming practice, it is recommended that in order to have peaceful dreams, you imagine yourself in the center of a *red* lotus and focus on the sound *ah*. This practice is designed to bring awareness to the unconscious workings of the mind and, in that awareness, transform the role of self from a victim of the "monkey mind," into a self-determined agent.

I finally understood my connection to the color red when I stepped into the color one day by surrounding myself with orange-red fabric. I felt calm and vitalized. I remembered this same feeling when I was in Tibet, and I would walk into meditation centers for monks and nuns where the overriding color would be the deep-red, long, curtainlike fabrics draped from the ceilings and the red of their habits. Red has the longest light wavelengths on the color spectrum, and it is known to be calming during meditation. In the East, red is associated with the first of the energy centers called chakras, located near the tail of the spine. I wondered if red was used to help meditators calm their racing thoughts. Yet I also knew it could stimulate the brain and ignite passion. It is the color of fire and of molten lava as it comes out of the earth. Fire-red catalyzes, adds energy, and clears a pathway for something new. I concluded that red represented to me the unfettered vitality of life that transcends "rational thought." For me, a red lotus, which I drew below, was a symbol of the fire and power of the feminine, clearing away the clutter of the patriarchy to make a vitalizing call for the creation and continuation of a loving and beautiful life.

ELLE'S SYMBOL OF FEMININE POWER

One day, I had a dream where I was walking down a long hallway with a bodyguard. He was tall, strong, and walked close to me. I felt safe with him. We went to the hair salon because I wanted to get my hair done. My bodyguard picked me up with his strong arms and set me down into one of the big swivel chairs. We looked around the salon, but didn't see anyone to do my hair. My bodyguard reached into his pocket and pulled out a long, pink satin ribbon. He took a lock of my hair, combed it with his big hands, and very gently began braiding the ribbon into my hair.

This dream represents my new relationship with my internal masculine as a result of doing this work. My inner misogynist is now a loving, kind bodyguard who treats me with respect, love, and protection. To me, this is both the definition and the gift of Feminine Power.

At the center of your story, you receive your own resources because you have relaxed your defenses and released any blocks to your own generative, feminine energy. As you continue to find your true voice, a wellspring of inner fulfillment will become abundantly, endlessly available to you.

Feminine Power is the electric energy that you get when you have unleashed unity and harmony in your story.

"IF THERE EVER COMES A TIME WHEN THE WOMEN OF THE WORLD COME TOGETHER PURELY AND SIMPLY FOR THE BENEFIT OF MANKIND, IT WILL BE A FORCE SUCH AS THE WORLD HAS NEVER KNOWN."

MATTHEW ARNOLD
POET

PART FIVE

WHERE WE GO
FROM HERE

"WHEN A GREAT SHIP IS IN HARBOR AND MOORED, IT IS SAFE, THERE CAN BE NO DOUBT. BUT THAT IS NOT WHAT GREAT SHIPS ARE BUILT FOR."

DR. CLARISSA PINKOLA ESTÉS
AUTHOR

Together, we are creating a world that celebrates women's voices, stories, and lives.

It is time for you to implement change in your life, your community, and the world by exercising your own Feminine Power. The path may be clear for you, or you may want some direction. Below are ideas to make your own.

"THE PLAIN FACT IS THAT THE PLANET DOES
NOT NEED MORE SUCCESSFUL PEOPLE. BUT IT
DOES DESPERATELY NEED MORE PEACEMAKERS,
HEALERS, RESTORERS, STORYTELLERS,
AND LOVERS OF EVERY KIND. IT NEEDS
PEOPLE WHO LIVE WELL IN THEIR PLACES. IT
NEEDS PEOPLE OF MORAL COURAGE WILLING TO JOIN
THE FIGHT TO MAKE THE WORLD HABITABLE AND
HUMANE. AND THESE QUALITIES HAVE LITTLE
TO DO WITH SUCCESS AS WE HAVE DEFINED IT."

DAVID W. ORR
PROFESSOR

LOVE

APPRECIATE OUR GENDER

Advocate for other women. Don't forget the past and the women who fought for equality. Educate yourself about the lives of other women, including their travails and the ways they have overcome them. Seek counsel from other women, especially elders. For the women you know well, remind them of their dreams and beauty. Revel in being with women and sharing in their knowledge. Advocate for younger women and join mentor programs or become a tutor for girls in your neighborhood and beyond.

FEED THE FUTURE

Join nonprofit organizations that combat hunger. Volunteer, donate money, or help with publicity and fund-raising. Fifteen percent of the United States population lives below the poverty line. When you count children alone, the number increases to 20 percent. Now is the time to bring your love forward and do what you can to help children and families meet basic food needs. Beyond the United States, the situation gets worse. Sadly, millions of children are at risk of starvation around the globe.

LOVE YOUR BODY

Revel in how your body sustains you. Note how it is engineered to help you move around, get your needs met, hold others, and heal itself. What does your body need? When you look in the mirror, be kind to yourself and find beauty in what you see despite any critical inner voices. Make sure to get health and medical care. When you care for your body, it will provide for you and for the people you want to help.

LOVE YOUR RESTFUL MIND

Did you know that stress actually damages your DNA? Dr. Elizabeth Blackburn discovered that stress directly impacts our telomeres, the protective end caps on our chromosomes, which are essential for preserving our genetic information. If your telomeres are not maintained, you can lose your protective shield against aging and diseases, such as cancer. Learn to meditate. Meditation promotes internal happiness, stronger brain functioning, and the capacity to stay attentive. Download an app that will help you meditate for just five minutes a day. Love your restful mind and the practices that allow you to find calm no matter where you are in your day.

LOVE YOUR WHOLE BEING BY SEEKING HELP WHEN YOU NEED IT

The work presented in this book may trigger memories or feelings that you aren't familiar with and might bring up more questions than you can answer. This may be a signal to ask for the assistance of others. This is a great practice. In general, it is important to get help when you need it—and even when you just want it. If you are feeling challenged for whatever reason, reach out to others, like a medical professional, therapist, social worker, or spiritual counselor.

AMPLIFY WOMEN'S VOICES

During the Obama administration, female White House staffers began noticing that their voices were often drowned out or their ideas were co-opted by male colleagues. "So female staffers adopted a strategy for meetings that they called 'amplification,'" Juliet Eilperin writes. She describes the strategy: "When a woman made a key point, other women would repeat it, giving credit to its author. This forced the men in the room to recognize the contribution—and denied them the chance to claim the idea as their own." The strategy worked, and President Obama took notice, calling on more women during staff meetings.

CELEBRATE THE MEN WHO FIGHT FOR EQUALITY

The Women's March on January 21, 2017, was the largest single-day protest in United States history. Among many reasons for marching—advocating for racial justice, reproductive rights, LGBTQ rights, and immigration reform—one of the rallying points was the distress many felt about the election of Donald Trump as the forty-fifth president, whose past words and actions were misogynistic. The Women's March crushed all expectations, and worldwide participation was estimated at five million people. All over the globe, many men joined the women, carrying extraordinary signs, too, and wearing unforgettable T-shirts, reminding everyone that when women's rights are celebrated, everyone wins.

"I CALL MYSELF A FEMI

NIST.

"ISN'T THAT WHAT YOU CALL SOMEONE WHO FIGHTS FOR WOMEN'S RIGHTS?"

THE DALAI LAMA

VOTE WOMEN INTO LEADERSHIP POSITIONS EVERYWHERE

Join organizations that support women who aspire to positions of political leadership. Almost 15,000 women are now running for office with help from nonprofit organizations. Work on their campaigns and vote for them. Run for office if you feel called. Ask for what you need. Women who care will support you.

CREATIVE NONVIOLENT CAMPAIGNS

In the classic play *Lysistrata*, women in ancient Greece refused to have sex with their husbands until they ended the Peloponnesian War. Inspired by the story, modern-day women in a small village, Sirt, in Turkey, refused to have sex with their husbands until they got running water. They got running water.

When Vice President-elect Mike Pence publicly denounced a woman's right to choose, more than 80,000 people responded by donating to Planned Parenthood. When filling out the online donation form that asked "Who is making this donation?" more than 20,000 people wrote in "Mike Pence."

ADVOCATE FOR APPROPRIATE REPRESENTATIONS OF WOMEN IN THE MEDIA

- *If you choose not to watch a movie or TV show because of violence, use your social media accounts to ask others to boycott it with you, explaining that the show contains violence against women.*

- *Vote with your dollars and support companies that use healthy-looking models in their advertisements.*

- *Advocate for more films showcasing female power, especially those that feature women over the age of 50!*

- *Celebrate your sexuality and wear what you want to wear.*

- *Celebrate your femininity in any way you want, and when you see a woman who has exuberantly stepped out to celebrate her love of self, compliment her!*

DANCE

SUSIE:

A few years ago I started taking a dance class that combines hula, belly, and African dance forms, all of which primarily use hip movements. When I was dancing and moving my hips, I remembered, when I was in high school, my grandmother was horrified that I wanted to study belly dancing because it was considered "cheap" and "too sexy." Yet as an adult in this class, I had an enlivening and restorative feeling that would stay with me throughout the day. It boosted my self-esteem and energized me. The more I did this class, the more these powerful feelings would fill me. It was like a homecoming for my body. I concluded that in my white, middle-class culture, the hip was the lost body part. Dancing brought this crucial part of the female anatomy, the place that cradles life, back to me.

TEND AND BEFRIEND

SUPPORT THOSE WHO SUPPORT WOMEN

Just as the Grameen Bank discovered, women tend to take care of others when they have the resources; they put the money they make back into their communities to make them healthier. Roll up your sleeves and help women get access to resources they can use to tend to others.

- *Support women in your community who are trying to get jobs or citizenship by providing a reference or personal letter.*

- *Volunteer your time or donate money to organizations that fight misogyny, such as domestic violence shelters and rape crisis hotlines.*

- *Support female artists—singers, painters, choreographers, filmmakers.*

- *Vote women into leadership positions. Women's natural tendencies to connect and engage make them outstanding leaders.*

FOSTER UNDERSTANDING AND FORGIVENESS

When people begin to understand the limited nature of living in a patriarchal world, some may feel ashamed of their unwitting participation in it. They might start to feel angry or sad about the things they have said or done that have perpetuated this dominating paradigm that has caused so much damage. Mothers and fathers may feel this about messages they've given their young daughters and sons. If someone publicly acknowledges this realization, it can be a moment of transformation. Your job is to support, not to shame.

"FORGIVING AND BEING RECONCILED
TO OUR ENEMIES OR OUR LOVED
ONES IS NOT ABOUT PRETENDING THAT
THINGS ARE OTHER THAN THEY
ARE. IT IS NOT ABOUT PATTING ONE
ANOTHER ON THE BACK AND TURNING
A BLIND EYE TO THE WRONG.
TRUE RECONCILIATION EXPOSES THE
AWFULNESS, THE ABUSE, THE HURT,
THE TRUTH. IT COULD EVEN SOMETIMES
MAKE THINGS WORSE.
IT IS A RISKY UNDERTAKING, BUT IN
THE END IT IS WORTHWHILE, BECAUSE
IN THE END ONLY AN HONEST
CONFRONTATION WITH REALITY CAN
BRING REAL HEALING.
SUPERFICIAL RECONCILIATION CAN BRING
ONLY SUPERFICIAL HEALING."

DESMOND TUTU
HEAD OF THE TRUTH AND RECONCILIATION
COMMISSION IN SOUTH AFRICA

For example, Susie sent an email to her father confronting him about his anger toward her mother, which seemed out of proportion. The disdain he expressed toward her mom reminded her of misogyny. The email was instigated by his angry complaint that his wife had betrayed the marriage when she started planning her own birthday party with her sister without informing him. Susie considered this absurd. Because the party was three months away, she had plenty of time to fill him in, and as far as Susie knew, he had only planned a birthday party for her once in his life. For her father to call this a betrayal seemed over the top, and Susie articulated, in angry and clear terms, that she found her father's behavior insulting, belittling, and part of a pattern of disrespect for both his wife and his daughter. This email exchange happened during the time that Susie was coming to terms with her own inner misogynist. Amazingly, Susie's father replied to her email with a genuine apology. Not only that, he told Susie that he was grateful that she felt brave enough to say something. He said:

Susie was stunned and amazed at his response. She didn't expect it, but later it occurred to her that since she had worked long and hard on her own issues, the confidence in her approach was different from the many times she attempted to change his behavior before. She had practiced interacting with an even scarier misogynist than her father, her inner self, so her voice was clear and her words definite. Their relationship was transformed for the better after that. Years later, for his 75th birthday, Susie wrote a song for him that celebrated the insights and changes he had made in his life to support not only his wife but also his daughter, granddaughter, and other women. After Susie's father's death, his caregiver told Susie that twice a week he would listen to that song, sing along, and cry.

Susie's dad once said:

> *"You know, I came from a chauvinistic kind of family and so did my wife. So I thought it was normal. We both thought it was normal. But the turning point was when I got Susie's email calling me on my behavior. At first I was going to defend myself, but then my wife reminded me that Susie had really put herself on the line to tell me how she felt and I should take in what she had written. She was right. And in that moment, I could hear the truth. "*

—Jim Herrick

LEAD

IDENTIFY AND HONOR EVERYDAY HEROINES AMONG US

You most likely encounter women every day, everywhere you go. Celebrate the amazing women you see, work with, and know. Acknowledge other women's ideas, desires, and contributions. Make it a ritual to tell other women when you notice the marvelous things they do.

SHARE FEMININE INTELLIGENCE

Tell your story. Use it to inspire others. Be proud of the insights you've gained and, when you see the opportunity, consider that another woman is longing to have access to the knowledge that you have gained.

Bring back and support repressed feminine wisdom from the past, such as:

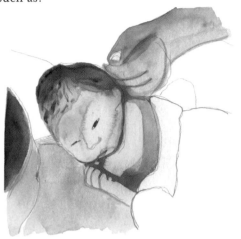

NATURAL BIRTH PRACTICES

PARTICIPATING IN PUBLIC
SERVICE AND HELPING
THE DISADVANTAGED
AND ELDERLY AMONG US

PLANT MEDICINE

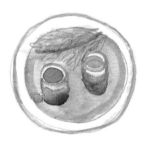

WOMEN'S CIRCLES

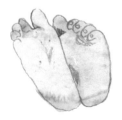

FAMILY RITUALS

SHARED CRAFTS
(SEWING CIRCLES)

CONNECTING WITH AND
RELATING TO YOUR
COMMUNITY AND
NEIGHBORS

Stories live inside you and shape your life. Be your own new story. Right here, right now, you get to choose what you want your story to be about!

"We are the curators

of life on earth."

HELEN CALDICOTT
ANTI-NUCLEAR ADVOCATE

Peacemakers will reawaken their minds to their own code of ethics by allowing themselves to have needs and opinions. If you are a Peacemaker, as you discover what you really think, you will become motivated to come forth and act boldly in life to advocate for the things you love.

THE PEACEMAKER
TYPE NINE

THE CHALLENGER
TYPE EIGHT

When Challengers relax the fear that makes them want to be bigger and stronger than others, they reawaken the child within themselves. If you are a Challenger, know your connection to your own brave, generous, and magnanimous heart, and your powerful vulnerability and innocence will ripple throughout your community.

THE ENTHUSIAST
TYPE SEVEN

When Enthusiasts run toward pain and away from gluttony, they gain sobriety, a sense of surefootedness, and a deep-rooted feeling of joy. If you are an Enthusiast, acknowledge your pain and the difficult parts of life, and you will be a beacon of joy and fulfillment for everyone you meet.

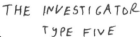

THE TROUBLESHOOTER
TYPE SIX

When Troubleshooters understand that there will never be guaranteed safety, they remember their heart, they remember what they love, and they begin to find their own courage within. If you are a Troubleshooter, notice what is in your heart and feel the warmth there. Let it guide you.

THE INVESTIGATOR
TYPE FIVE

When Investigators realize that they have collected enough information, they relax their need for knowledge and find their own innate voice. If you are an Investigator, lead with your intuition.

THE REFORMER
TYPE ONE

When Reformers judge themselves less, they will start to emanate the glow of loving themselves fully. If you are a Reformer, remember that serenity is a precious aspect for other women to experience in you.

THE CARETAKER
TYPE TWO

When Caretakers start to prioritize their own needs and relax their need to be "the loving one," their hearts open to humility and abundant love. If you are a Caretaker, become an example of someone who is comfortable taking care of her needs without shame.

THE ACHIEVER
TYPE THREE

When Achievers relax their need to inflate their own image, they gain authenticity and truth because they start to experience their own vast and honest potential. If you are an Achiever, share your truth so that we will all experience what we need—your true depth and value.

THE INDIVIDUALIST
TYPE FOUR

When Individualists start to remember that the grass is greener not on the other side of the fence, but inside of themselves, they experience a deep sense of their own significance and find balance. If you are an Individualist, share the equanimity that you have found within so that we can all experience its beauty and significance.

THE ULTIMATE TASK,
WHICH YOU HAVE
ACCOMPLISHED WITH
THIS BOOK, IS TO FIND
LOVE FOR YOURSELF
SO THAT YOU CAN
RELEASE YOUR FEARS
OF THE PATRIARCHY.
WITH THIS LOVE,
YOU RECOGNIZE THAT
YOU ARE THE WOMAN
THAT YOU LONG TO BE.
AND WHEN YOU
REACH YOUR HEART,
YOU BRING ALL OF US
WITH YOU.

One night, Susie had a dream:

I walked out onto a beach that looked wild and restless, like it could be in northern Scotland. Everything was dark—it was a moonless night, the sand was a volcanic dark gray, and the water reflected the darkness. There was a boat with people in it near where the water and sand met, and I got into the boat. After settling in, before we pushed off to sea, I turned to discover that a huge tsunami was coming toward us. Astonished and terrified, I looked at the people in the boat to warn them and noticed that they were all women. "Don't worry!" one of the women said, and together, we began to maneuver the boat, passing safely through the curl of the wave, coming out the other side together.

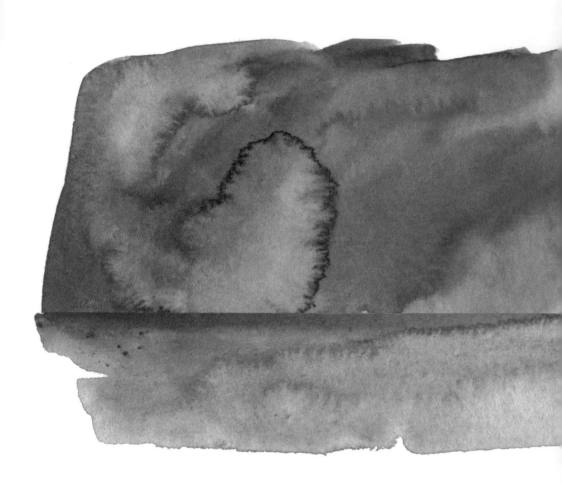

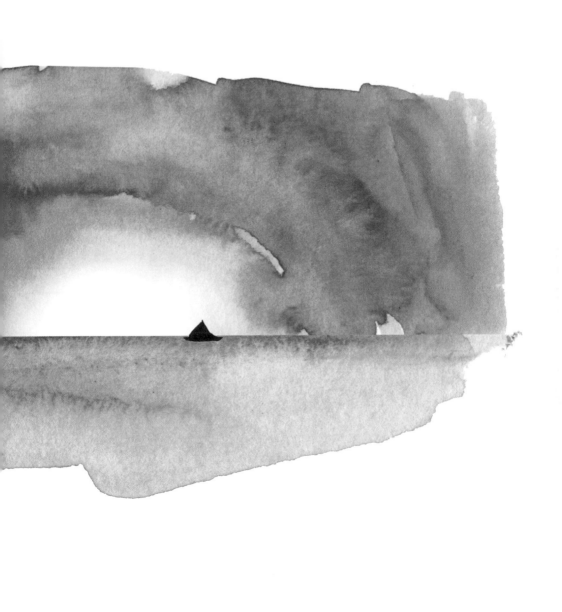

ACKNOWLEDGMENTS

We would both like to thank Mary Ellen O'Neill, our guardian angel editor. Mary Ellen, we love you! Thank you for breathing life into every page of this manuscript. You are so talented at what you do, and we are eternally grateful to have cocreated this book with you. Thank you Ted Weinstein, our literary agent and a skilled matchmaker, for supporting us in finding a marvelous publishing partner for this book! We would also like to thank Michael Naylor, for sharing his exquisite wisdom of the Enneagram, and Christine Hooker and Louann Brizendine, for their neuroscience expertise. Finally, we would like to thank the entire Workman team for helping to shape this offering and launch it into the world to create positive impact.

Susie would like to thank: Elle, who bravely walked this path with me, never flagging, never losing faith, always believing in the intelligence of two hearts wanting to save the world. Your practice of finding and sharing your unfettered artistic soul is the light I work by. My mom, who has a steadfast optimism that saves my soul. Jill, who showed me where the jewels lie in the waking dream of life. Brad, who lives by example, by committing to love me continuously and unconditionally, and to share in the task of helping the feminine re-emerge in the most deliciously masculine way.

Elle would like to thank: Thank you, Susie, for sharing this path—both on the page and in life—where it blooms in full color. Thank you for living and writing *Aphrodite Emerges,* and for offering the gems you discovered, along with your powerful therapeutic expertise, as a template for this book. We did it because you bravely did it first. Thank you, Mom and Dad, for showing me the power of unconditional love and always believing in me. And thank you to Tessa, Zoey, Twyla, Austin, CCii, Center Sky, Circa Luna, Lilly, Erica, Elise, Kate, Mabel, Tenzin, Skyler, and Josie—the future of Feminine Power is bright!

A NOTE ON THE TYPE

This book is set in Mrs Eaves, designed by Zuzana Licko in 1966. It was chosen for Ms. Licko's dedication to an "overall openness and lightness." Of the name, she says, "This typeface is named after Sarah Eaves, the woman who became John Baskerville's wife. As Baskerville was setting up his printing and type business, Mrs. Eaves moved in with him as a live-in housekeeper, eventually becoming his wife after the death of her first husband, Mr. Eaves. Like the widows of Caslon, Bodoni, and the daughters of Fournier, Sarah similarly completed the printing of the unfinished volumes that John Baskerville left upon his death." (Quoted from the 1996 type specimen booklet for Mrs Eaves titled "More Mrs Eaves.")

ABOUT THE AUTHORS

ELLE LUNA is a designer, painter, writer, and the author of *The Crossroads of Should and Must*. She facilitates a global art movement, #The100DayProject, where participants create and post something every day for 100 days, and she speaks to groups around the world, sharing the story of *The Crossroads of Should and Must*. Ms. Luna lives in the San Francisco Bay Area and online at elleluna.com and @ElleLuna on Instagram.

SUSIE HERRICK is a licensed psychotherapist, Enneagram teacher, mediator, trainer, and consultant, as well as the author of *Aphrodite Emerges*. She has taught, coached, and mentored thousands of graduate students in counseling psychology. Ms. Herrick lives in the San Francisco Bay Area. Learn more at SusieHerrick.com and AphroditeEmerges.com.

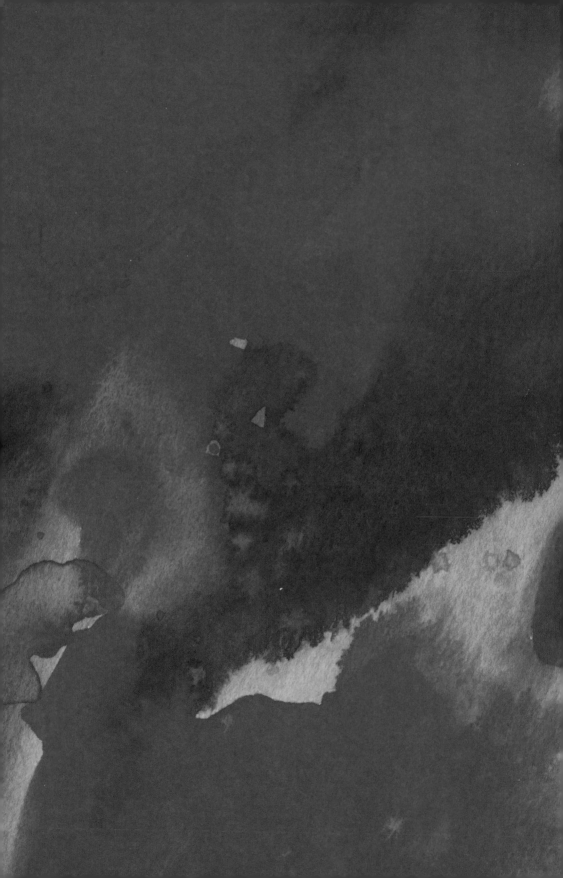